BUY YOUR
FIRST HOME
NOW

BUY YOUR FIRST HOME NOW

A Practical Guide to Better Deals, Cheaper Mortgages, and Bigger Tax Breaks for the First-Time Home Buyer

Peter G. Miller

1817

HARPER & ROW, PUBLISHERS, New York

Grand Rapids, Philadelphia, St. Louis, San Francisco

London, Singapore, Sydney, Tokyo, Toronto

FIRST EDITION

Library of Congress Cataloging-in-Publication Data

Miller, Peter G.
    Buy your first home now : a practical guide to better deals,
  cheaper mortgages, and bigger tax breaks for the first-time home
  buyer / Peter G. Miller.—1st ed.
      p. cm.
    ISBN 0-06-016233-3
    1. House buying. 2. Mortgage loans. 3. Real property and
  taxation. 4. Real estate business.   I. Title.
  HD1379.M5967   1990

90 91 92 93 94 CC/HC 10 9 8 7 6 5 4 3 2 1

To Merri, Walter,
and Stephanie Rae

Contents

Acknowledgments

This book would not have been possible without the assistance of many individuals and organizations. I wish to thank Jeff Lubar, Liz Duncan, and Walter Molony of the National Association of Realtors; Curt Culver and Lori Stahl at the Mortgage Guarantee Insurance Corporation; Judy Estey with Coldwell Banker; Jerry Karbon of the Credit Union National Association; George Rosenberg with *Who's Who in Creative Real Estate;* Richard G. Wood and the Home Owners Warranty Corporation; and Valery Greene and the National Cooperative Bank.

I would also like to thank information officers associated with the Census Bureau, the Veterans Administration, the Department of Housing and Urban Development, the Internal Revenue Service, and the Federal Housing Administration.

Portions of the first chapter have been published privately by the author within an analysis of the real estate marketing system.

Portions of the first guideline in Chapter 15 appeared originally in material written and published privately by the author.

Portions of the material in Chapter 17 originally appeared in the July/August issue of *The Real Estate Professional* (Wellesley Publications, Inc., 1492 Highland Avenue, Needham, MA 02192).

Portions of Chapter 1 concerning real estate prices and population originally appeared in the November/December 1989 issue of *The Real Estate Professional.*

The glossary includes both new material as well as definitions which have appeared in *The Common-Sense Mortgage, Successful Real Estate Negotiation,* and *Successful Real Estate Investing.* I wish to thank my negotiation co-author, Douglas M. Bregman, Esq., of Bethesda, MD, for allowing my use of the negotiation definitions in this book.

This is my fourth real estate book with Harper & Row, a project which would not have been possible without the ideas, advice, and encouragement of my editor, Terry Karten, and the many people involved in the magical transformation of a basic manuscript into the book you now hold. I am enormously grateful to them all.

Preface

There is a visible inequity in America, an unfairness that transcends generations.

By every measure we are well-housed, but for too many of us the roof over our heads is owned by someone else. There are people in every state who simply cannot buy a basic home in a reasonable location, despite the fact that they work, are responsible, and want just as much as anyone to have the option of homeownership.

This is a book for and about first-time buyers and the steps you can take to achieve homeownership. It not only follows from my experience buying property, but also from my experience as a broker and educator who has helped others.

We live in a society where television shows us that everything from domestic conflicts to complex crimes can be resolved in 30 minutes. Homebuying should be so simple, but it isn't.

This is not a book that pretends homeownership is easy to achieve or that cash and income are unnecessary. Rather it suggests that with study and hard work, first-time buyers can often reduce the need for capital, substitute guarantees for cash, borrow money even with limited incomes, and find homes that represent good deals today and excellent potential tomorrow.

This book contains no substitute for hard work, no shortcuts for study and education. It assumes that buying a first home is complex and that the best way to achieve homeownership is to pursue those alternatives and options which are reasonable in today's marketplace.

The path from casual interest to binding contracts to actual ownership is neither neat nor tidy. But there is a pattern of events which most first-time buyers encounter, a pattern that is reflected in the organization of this book. We move from general issues to specific strategies, analyzing each topic from the buyer's perspective.

This book is designed to be a consumer-oriented handbook for first-time buyers, a seminar text, and a practical reference for brokers and agents. It follows in form and concept the three earlier books in this series, *The Common-Sense Mortgage*, *Successful Real Estate Negotiation* (with Douglas M. Bregman), and *Successful Real Estate Investing.*

To those who read these words I wish every success. At one point those who now own homes were first-time buyers, and with dedication, energy, and study you too can join their ranks.

Peter G. Miller
Silver Spring, MD

BUY YOUR FIRST HOME NOW

1

The Generation Divide: Why Houses Cost So Much

Each year millions of homes are bought and sold, but for many people such events are irrelevant. Housing is expensive, income is limited, and savings are thin. While a home is desirable, the demands of modern life—the cost of food, transportation, shelter, clothing, taxes—ensure that for many prospective purchasers homeownership is something in the future. Maybe.

Today we have millions of people who are not unhoused or ill-housed, they are simply non-owners. They rent at an age when their parents bought, rent at a time when others are buying, rent in an era when tax policies encourage ownership, rent while owners build equity, and rent in an environment where housing offers the best possible hedge against inflation and taxes.

The issue is not that renting is terrible, or that rental properties cannot offer valued features or a comfortable lifestyle. The problem is that for many who prefer to buy, ownership is less and less plausible each day.

Why? In basic terms, both housing expenses and money costs have shot up. Together, these two central costs have outpaced the ability of many people to finance real estate.

Consider my experience. My homeownership history parallels that of many individuals now in their 40s. My experience also explains why people in their 20s and 30s have so much difficulty buying a first house.

I bought my first house in 1973 and in rough terms the deal worked like this: I paid $36,000 and financed my purchase with

1

a fixed-rate loan at 7 percent interest. I put down $3,600 (10 percent) and found a $32,400 mortgage. The monthly payment for principal and interest was just $215.56.

Nobody would mistake my first home for a grand chateau or a European palace. As a single adult in my mid-20s, I bought what I could afford, what the real estate industry might call a "starter" home. Located in the Maryland suburbs outside Washington, D.C., it was a brick house with three bedrooms, a central bath, and a nice yard. It was also a house that I sold in three years with an $8,000 profit.

Today the same property is probably worth $145,000, and the deal I made is impossible. (See Table 1.)

- I put down $3,600. Today's higher value will require a down payment of $14,500 if 90 percent financing is available.

- My initial mortgage principal was $32,400. With 90 percent financing, a $130,500 loan will be required today.

- My monthly payments for principal and interest were $215.56. If the interest rate is now 10.5 percent, the payments for a 30-year, $130,500 loan will amount to $1,193.73 per month.

- When I bought, a purchaser could qualify for a $32,000 mortgage with an income from $13,000 to $16,000. Under today's standards, someone with a $1,200 monthly mortgage payment must earn more than $50,000 to buy my first house.

- Although I was hardly a candidate for the upper class when I bought my first home, it was affordable. In contrast, not only is housing expensive today, but ownership costs are over-

Table 1   HOW REAL ESTATE COSTS HAVE CHANGED: A PERSONAL EXAMPLE

	1973	*1989*
Purchase Price	$36,000	$145,000
10 Percent Down Payment	$3,600	$14,500
Loan Amount	$32,400	$130,500
Interest Rate	7 percent	10.5 percent
Monthly Payment (P & I)	$215.56	$1,193.73
Qualifying Income	$13,000+	$50,000+

whelming. When I bought in 1973, a typical 30-year-old purchaser devoted 21 percent of his or her income to housing
costs, according to a study by Frank Levy and Richard C.
Michel developed for the Joint Economic Committee of the
U.S. Congress. By 1984, the same study showed that 30-year-
old purchasers allocated 44 percent of their income for housing
expenses.

- If values rose from $36,000 to $145,000 over a 16-year period,
then the compounded appreciation rate for my property was
9.1 percent annually. Good, but not as good as many areas
where values have risen at an even faster pace.

    Coldwell Banker, for example, reports that prices for a typi-
cal three-bedroom house rose 6.2 percent nationwide in 1988,
but that far greater increases could be found in such diverse
urban areas as Allentown, Pennsylvania (24.1 percent), Belle-
vue, Washington (18 percent), Fort Wayne, Indiana (18 percent), Baltimore (11.6 percent), Washington, D.C. (11.8
percent inside the Beltway), and San Francisco (24.4 percent).
In San Marino, California, prices rose 55.3 percent!

    The problem with ongoing appreciation is that such increases
represent mixed blessings. If you're an owner, appreciation is
great. But if you're a buyer, the appreciation which seems so
attractive to sellers translates into steeper mortgage costs and the
need for more money at closing.

THE NATIONAL PATTERN

My experience is hardly unique. Those who bought 20, 15, or 10
years ago are ahead. Those trying to buy today face severe problems. Surveys, studies, and woeful stories all suggest that
homebuying is tough today and likely to become far more difficult in the future.

    In 1988, the percentage of first-time buyers who qualified for
a typical starter home was lower than in any year since 1975,
according to the National Association of Realtors (NAR). Among
prospective first-time buyers, fewer than 80 percent could afford
a home priced at $76,670. Whether safe and habitable properties
priced below $77,000 actually exist in or near many urban cen-
ters is an open question.

Fewer and fewer first-time purchasers can buy property because real estate values have consistently outpaced the consumer price index (CPI). Between 1968 and 1988, according to NAR figures, median sale prices for existing homes rose from $20,100 to $89,300, an annual increase of 7.74 percent. Meanwhile the cost of living during the same period rose from an index of 38.8 in 1968 to 118.3 in 1988, according to the Labor Department, an annual rise of 5.73 percent.

In practical terms, a house that cost $30,000 in 1966 should sell for $91,469 at the end of 1988 if housing prices increased at the same rate as the CPI. At the rate home values *actually* increased the same house today is likely to be worth $133,248, a figure remarkably close to that paid by the average buyer in many areas around the country. According to Coldwell Banker, a typical home with 2,000 square feet of living space cost $133,937 in a "mid-priced" housing area at the end of 1988.

THE MULTIPLIER EFFECT

As we have seen, over a period of years cash prices for housing rose just a little faster than consumer prices. While the gap between prices and housing was not especially large on an annual basis, over time the difference became significant.

More important, however, has been the effect of leverage. My $36,000 house rose in value over 16 years until it was worth $145,000. Comparing numbers, this property's value grew 9.1 percent each year.

But the truth is that I, like most homebuyers, never paid the full purchase price. I paid $3,600 in cash and I borrowed the rest. Since I had to live somewhere, the mortgage payments I made (and the interest I did not receive on my $3,600) were the economic equivalent of rent.

If you compare my $3,600 investment with a $109,000 value increase over 16 years, then the real appreciation rate was 23.76 percent.

The results seen with my property are not particularly unusual. Many people around the country have done as well, or better, and because such results are common, many individuals in their forties, fifties, sixties, and seventies today have substantial assets, while those in their twenties and thirties do not.

MORE HOMES, LESS HOUSING

Between 1971 and 1988, the number of owner-occupied houses grew from 41.8 million to 58.7 million, according to the Census Bureau, and the net result was that 16.9 million owner-occupied units were added to the housing stock.

Census figures also show how we filled these units. We created 26.3 million new households.

The problem is that the owner-occupied housing stock did not expand enough. Nearly 17 million new homes is a lot of real estate, but the formation of 26.3 million new households in the same period meant that 9.4 million families, couples, and individuals could not buy single-family housing. Too few houses coupled with too many households is a major reason why housing prices have soared in the past two decades.

UNSEEN HURDLES

Problems such as pricing, interest rates, and supply are clear and visible issues that are easy to follow and assess. Less noticeable, but no less important, are quiet practices which severely reduce housing availability.

Zoning. We usually think of zoning as positive community efforts to control the use of land. With zoning we can be sure that nobody builds a nuclear dump next door or that our neighbors do not locate an all-night go-go club in their basement.

But zoning also has a negative impact in the sense that land control also means limitations. If we zone an area so that minimum lot sizes are restricted to 10,000 square feet, we are limiting the number of homes that can be built in a given area and thus the housing supply. If we have zoning that says only single-family houses can be built, then we may well wind up with a community where some individuals or small families rattle around in enormous houses, while those who cannot afford such expensive settings must continue to rent.

There is now some pressure around the country to modify local zoning rules with such approaches as accessory apartments (allowing the creation of an additional living unit in "single-family" houses) and higher building densities (permitting more homes per acre). Each approach lowers housing costs.

There is also pressure to modify zoning rules in a different manner. Around the country many jurisdictions are looking at building moratoriums to hold down growth. Such moratoriums limit supply and therefore drive up prices.

Impact Fees.   Few issues are more touchy than taxes, so to raise additional revenue many jurisdictions have turned instead to *impact fees.*

Impact fees work like this: Stevens builds ten houses in the Heartland district. Since ten additional families will now settle in the area, it follows that there will be more children in school, more wear on local roads, more picnics in public parks, etc. To compensate for this additional use of public facilities, Heartland charges Stevens $2,000 for each house he builds. Stevens, of course, promptly raises his prices by at least $2,000, and the net result is more expensive new housing.

Impact fees also influence existing home values. If new housing is only available for $100,000 and impact fees add another $2,000 to the price, housing costs are being pushed up. Since prospective buyers can purchase either new homes or existing ones, if new construction prices rise, so will values for existing properties.

Impact fees, which can add as much as $10,000 in development costs per unit, are politically attractive because unlike sale or income levies, they are not seen as taxes—unless you're the one looking for a new home.

Status.   In the typical case first-time buyers are people who tend to be young or relatively young, individuals between the ages of 25 and 44.

Youth may have its rewards, but easy success in the housing market is not one of them. Many first-time buyers are single, and being single means there is no second income within the household to help support a mortgage. Other young purchasers may have recently started families, a time with extensive costs and great pressures.

Being young translates into early years on the career track, the very time when incomes are low because we are not yet established in our work. Being young also suggests that savings are lean because we've had little time to accumulate capital, the cash needed to buy a first house.

FUTURE TRENDS

So far we have seen that during the past two decades buying a first home has become increasingly difficult. As we look to the future, there are few trends that suggest an easier time for entry-level purchasers.

First, there is no evidence that housing prices around the country will decline radically except in the event of a national depression. If the national economy crashes, few people will have enough income to buy a first home anyway.

Prices for real estate are largely influenced by local trends rather than national economics, so we are likely to see three emerging patterns.

- In many areas prices will simply increase at or about the same rate as the cost of living. In such areas real property costs, as measured in buying power, will remain largely unchanged.
- Prices will decline in some areas as people move out, federal funds are withdrawn, commodity prices decline, or major businesses close.
- Prices will rise in areas where local economies are expanding. The best examples are likely to be such urban centers as Los Angeles and Washington, D.C.

Second, population changes, by themselves, will not reduce real estate values. Some economists have suggested that prices will fall substantially during the next two decades, in real terms and perhaps in cash terms as well, because the number of baby boomers entering the marketplace will decline.

In theory one would expect that as the number of buyers declines, demand will drop and therefore housing prices should weaken. In real life, there are convincing examples which show precisely the opposite effect.

For example, in 1970 the population of the District of Columbia totaled 757,000 people. By 1980, the District's population was down to 638,000 and the 1990 census will show a smaller population still.

Given a substantially smaller population one would expect District housing values to plummet—if the economic models are right. In real life, housing prices have shot up much faster than the rate of inflation.

We can also address the missing baby boomer theory by looking at Florida. The population there rose from nearly 6.8 million in 1970 to 12 million in 1987. With a huge population increase, prices might be expected to skyrocket but that has not happened. Most Florida real estate has, at best, appreciated at a leisurely pace, and there is no doubt that values have risen far faster in Washington, D.C. than in the Sunshine State.

While population influences real estate values, it is certainly not the central determining factor. If population is the key to housing values, than surely housing prices in Cairo would be far steeper than Los Angeles. The Egyptian capital's population density is ten times greater than that of the California city.

The key to housing values is the ability to afford given costs and the desire to own property in selected locations. Thus, if a community offers good jobs, people with incomes will compete for the best locations and prices will rise. In a community with few good jobs or a declining economic base, one would expect property values to remain stable relative to inflation or to actually fall.

If it's true that real estate values are going to fall because of selected population declines, then we might expect lenders to leave the mortgage business and find more profitable lines of work. After all, why give someone a 30-year loan secured with an asset that is likely to drop in value? If the value is certain to decline, then a borrower is better off giving back the property rather than repaying the loan, the precise conclusion reached by many Texas homeowners in the 1980s.

Alternatively, if real estate values will plummet, why permit borrowers to buy homes with 5 or 10 percent down? Surely lenders would be wise to demand more money from buyers up front, say 30 to 40 percent down.

Most lenders, obviously, have not left the mortgage business, at least not because they believe real estate values, and thus their security, will collapse. Rather than a trend toward huge down payments, lenders today appear ready and willing to make loans with 5 or 10 percent down.

As to the future, *housing will be cheap and plentiful in those areas where people don't want to live, where incomes are minimal, and where alternative housing choices are readily available.* In those areas which are desirable, where housing choices are limited, and where good jobs abound, real estate demand will continue and market values will remain strong.

2

The Need for Marketplace Equality

So far we have seen a housing market where virtually every condition, consideration, and custom is tilted against the first-time buyer. But as depressing as the housing situation may appear, prospective purchasers can take comfort from the fact that they are not pioneers. Brave souls have gone before, walked the same paths, faced the same problems, and ultimately won the coveted title of homeowner. You can do it too.

The real issue is not whether you can buy a house, but whether your first home will be a good deal—a property that makes sense in terms of pricing, financing, condition, comfort, and the potential for appreciation.

Making a good deal is not easy, but one step you can take to assure success is to enter the marketplace as an equal, or as equal as you can be, with the sellers, brokers, lenders, and others you will meet.

Striving for equality does not require the knowledge or insight of someone who has been in real estate for 20 years. What striving does suggest is that you will try to have a thorough understanding of the real estate marketing system and know how homes are priced, marketed, contracted, titled, conveyed, taxed, and financed. Striving for equality also means at least knowing which questions to ask, why the system works the way it does, who receives money for what, and how much they earn.

The more you know, the less dependent you will be on other

people, people whose interests naturally conflict with your own.
If taking time to learn about real estate seems hard, consider the
alternative. If you are forced to rely totally on sellers, their
agents, and a marketing system that greatly favors homeowners
rather than homebuyers, how will you get a good deal?

How do you become an equal?

First, recognize that everyone in the real estate field has
experience—except you. Brokers, lenders, and lawyers work real
estate deals every day, and their experience gives them an edge.
As for sellers, unless they inherited their property or married
someone with a home, they're ahead in the experience derby by
at least one deal.

Second, don't plan on buying tomorrow. The homebuying
process in the best circumstances will take several months and
often longer. Plan ahead and make sure you are not squeezed by
a need to move or other considerations.

Third, education is crucial. Read your local papers and magazines—there are excellent real estate sections throughout the
country. Clip and save those articles which offer tips and ideas
you can use. Attend courses and seminars, but be aware that
many programs are created primarily to generate business
rather than to merely educate first-time buyers.

Fourth, understand your marketplace position. You are a consumer searching for the best possible housing, financing, and
professional services. Other people in the marketplace, no matter how friendly, have different positions. Some, such as sellers,
are adversaries. They want higher prices and terms that favor
their interests. Others, such as brokers, lenders, and lawyers, are
business people who provide services in exchange for a fee. How
you buy and finance a home will directly influence their ability
to earn an income.

Fifth, be realistic. Your first property, like mine, is unlikely to
be either a castle or a penthouse suite. The point is to own
something you can use as a stepping stone to a better property
or enhanced economic freedom.

Sixth, listen. Speak to brokers, sellers, lawyers, lenders, and
recent purchasers. What are their ideas, strategies, opinions, and
experiences? What might work for you or save you money?

The time to start the homebuying process is now. It's unlikely that homebuying will become easier, that the marketing system will change, or that homes will become radically more affordable. Why wait?

KNOWLEDGE FIRST, OPEN HOUSES SECOND

Too often we see a house we love and visions of ownership flash before us. Why not? Homes are marketed on the basis of style, status, and ego. Emotions first, business second. Instant gratification with as little detail as possible, if you please. In such an environment, why shouldn't purchasers be blessed with a divine right of immediate possession?

Homebuying should be an emotional process, but it should also be seen as a business deal. As much as looking at homes seems right, natural, and fun, first-time buyers who venture into the marketplace unprepared are likely to encounter costly problems and great dissatisfaction.

As a first-time buyer, you can learn about real estate before you purchase a home, or afterward. If you buy a house first, if you're not an informed purchaser, the extra costs will haunt you for years to come.

Rather than looking at homes first, start with financing. Understand basic mortgage alternatives and you can tell which homes are affordable, which are not, and which loans represent the best possible deals.

3

Taxes and Ownership

The homebuying process is sufficiently awesome that even the most courageous person can become positively squeamish. In exchange for leaving a rental property where the work, headaches, and details of ownership are left to someone else, you are about to consider the purchase of living space where every break, crack, leak, chip, dent, weed, clog, stoppage, and outage is yours. Not only will you have more responsibility, you will also have the opportunity to regularly make major payments for mortgages, taxes, and insurance, opportunities you won't want to miss. Congratulations.

But if you're renting now, you should ask: Will I benefit from ownership? The difference between renting and ownership may be surprising, as it was to Mr. Clark.

April 15th is a special day for Clark, the day he and just about everyone else file their taxes. For Clark, the week before had evolved into a ritual time when Clark and his former college roommate met to help each other with an endless array of forms and schedules.

Clark and his friend—we'll call him Murphy—are the same age, are married, and earn the same income. Neither has dependents. The major difference between them is housing: Clark rents while Murphy owns a house.

Clark and his wife make $42,000 a year. They also spend $750 a month on rent, plus utilities. At tax time, Clark subtracts deductions for his wife and himself ($3,900 in 1988) plus a standardized amount, $5,000 in this case. Clark's taxable income, figured with 1988 rates, is $33,100 and his tax totals $5,408.

Murphy and his wife also share a $42,000 household income. Murphy owns a house bought for $97,250 and pays $900 a month for principal, interest, taxes, and insurance (PITI), a total of $10,800 a year. Of this amount, $1,000 is for property taxes and $200 for insurance. As for the 30-year, $87,500 mortgage at 10.5 percent interest, virtually the entire $800 monthly payment is interest—a little more than $9,100 a year.

When Murphy figures his taxes, he takes deductions for his wife and himself ($3,900), home mortgage interest ($9,100), char-

---

Four Reasons Not to Buy

Homebuying is not an activity to be taken lightly, and there are perfectly sane reasons why buying a home may not be appropriate at any given moment.

Transfers.   If it's likely that you will move during the next two to three years because of a job change, or for any other reason, the purchase of a home today may lead to losses. Even if the property appreciates, you still must pay acquisition costs up front and marketing costs when you sell, expenses that can quickly eat up profits.

Down Markets.   If local real estate prices are declining, then it may pay to stay away from the market until values begin to rebound. Look for local economic upswings to predict rising values, items reported in local papers such as lower unemployment, increased retail sale volume, and the opening of new roads, factories, office buildings, or malls.

Alternative Investments.   While homeownership can be attractive, your dollars may be better spent by investing in more education, professional equipment to advance your career, or the purchase of a business interest.

Inconsistent or Insufficient Income.   If your income is not steady, or there isn't enough of it, then homeownership may not be appropriate at this time.

itable contributions ($500), property taxes ($1,000), and state income taxes ($1,250). Murphy's taxable income: $26,250. Murphy's tax: $3,926.

INDIRECT TAX BENEFITS

When renting and buying are contrasted, it's not uncommon to hear only about tax write-offs for mortgage interest. Yet the fact is that homeownership may lead to deductions not even related to housing.

To see why, look at the forms used by Clark and Murphy. Clark used form 1040A, a form with no provision for itemized deductions. Had Clark used a form 1040, he would have been entitled to itemize, but the expenses he can write off—state income taxes and charitable deductions—are less than the $5,000 standard deduction to which he and Mrs. Clark are entitled.

Murphy, in contrast, has more than $5,000 in deductions, and rather than take the standardized deduction, he itemizes. By itemizing, Murphy can not only write off mortgage interest, he can also deduct property taxes, state income taxes, and charitable deductions. In certain cases, he might also be able to write off medical bills, theft losses, moving expenses, and miscellaneous items. (See Table 2.)

Table 2 DEDUCTIONS FOR CLARK AND MURPHY

	Clark	Murphy
Income	$42,000	$42,000
Personal Deductions (2)	$3,900	$3,900
Standardized Deduction	$5,000	0
Mortgage Interest	0	$9,100
Property Taxes	0	$1,000
Charity	0	$500
State Income Taxes	0	$1,250
Taxable Income	$33,100	$26,250
Taxes (1988)	$5,408	$3,926
Extra Tax	$1,482	0

Source: IRS Publication 17 (Revised Nov. 88).

When the two college friends looked at their tax bills the difference was significant. Clark paid $150 a month less for housing ($750 versus $900), but he also paid additional taxes worth $1,482 ($5,408 less $3,926), or $123.50 per month. In effect, Clark's apartment costs just $26.50 less per month than Murphy's home after taxes.

So far, our comparison between Murphy and Clark has looked only at *basic* monthly costs and taxes. To have a better comparison, we need to go further and address such issues as repairs, insurance, opportunity costs, and the possibility of appreciation.

REPAIRS

Housing is complex and repairs are an ongoing concern. Since every property needs repairs, it follows that owners should expect to face regular repair bills. As to how often repairs will be required, that's an open question that depends on the property's age, complexity (homes with more gadgets and appliances have more items to go wrong), and maintenance level (regular maintenance will hold down and sometimes eliminate costly repair bills), as well as the owner's ability and willingness to do some or all of the work.

For renters the situation is different. Some renters have no repair bills—repairs are assumed by the owner. If the owner is concerned about the property's condition and the ability to attract tenants, this is a great situation for renters.

Some tenants, however, are faced with less attractive situations.

First, there are leases that require tenants to make small repairs themselves, "small" perhaps being defined as items that cost less than $25 to fix. The owner pays everything over $25.

Second, some leases, especially those associated with single-family houses, may shift repair burdens entirely to tenants, sometimes in exchange for lower rental rates.

Third, there are owners who delay or ignore repair obligations. In such cases, owners simply save money, but at the cost of declining properties and unattractive living conditions for tenants.

For our analysis, let's assume that Clark has no repair expenses while owner Murphy pays $50 per month, or $600 per year, to maintain his property.

INSURANCE

The four major expenses faced by owner Murphy are mortgage principal, mortgage interest, taxes, and property insurance. We have not provided a property insurance cost for Clark because he has no real estate to insure.

But Clark may elect to carry renter's insurance, coverage that protects against the loss of personal belongings from fire, theft, and vandalism. In effect, such a policy is similar to homeowner's insurance except that structural damage is not covered.

Insurance is sometimes required by a lease, but whether required or not it's often a good idea. The annual cost for coverage worth $15,000 in many areas is no more than $125, so we'll say that Clark, like Murphy, insures his belongings and pays $125 per year.

OPPORTUNITY COSTS

An *opportunity cost* is a possible benefit lost by taking a particular action. If we spend $10 for a compact disc, we have lost the revenue that $10 might have made for us had we invested the money elsewhere.

In our example with Murphy and Clark, Clark rented and therefore did not need money for a down payment. Instead, he was required to make an up-front deposit, $750 in this case. At 10 percent interest, Clark is losing $75 each year the management holds his money. This loss is offset by deposit interest required by local rules, say 4 percent a year, or $30. In total, Clark loses $45 annually on his deposit.

Murphy bought his property for $97,250 and paid $12,000 at closing for a down payment and general settlement expenses. At 10 percent interest, Murphy has a $1,200 opportunity cost— money he could have earned had he not bought a house. If Clark also has $12,000 and puts it in an account at 10 percent interest, he will earn $1,200.

Table 3 shows that with reasonable assumptions for costs and

Table 3   RENTING VERSUS OWNERSHIP: CLARK VERSUS
MURPHY

Initial Cash Outlay	*Clark* *$750*	*Murphy* *$12,000*
Monthly Payment (PITI)	$750	$900
Annual Cost	$9,000	$10,800
Repairs	0	$600
Tax Savings	0	−$1,446
Deposit Interest Lost	$45	0
Insurance	$125	0
Opportunity Cost	−$1,200	$1,200
Amortization (First Year)	0	−$438
Appreciation (First Year)	0	−$6,807
Total Economic Cost	$7,970	$3,909
Monthly Economic Cost	$664.17	$325.75

benefits, the true economic expense of renting is twice as large
as the cost of ownership, $325.75 versus $664.17 per month.
While the fine points in our example are open to debate, the basic
conclusion is absolutely clear: In an environment where property
values are increasing, ownership is a far better deal than renting.

POSSIBLE APPRECIATION

Real estate values, as we saw in the first chapter, have generally
risen over the past 20 years. Let's assume that prices where
Murphy and Clark live are now rising 7 percent a year, not the
country's biggest increase, but better than those areas where
local economies have been stagnant or declining.

Murphy bought his property two years ago for $97,250. After
one year, the value increased by 7 percent, or $6,807. In the
second year, the value again increased by 7 percent, another
$7,284.

At this point the property Murphy bought for $97,250 is
worth $111,341 and his equity (market value less debt) stands at
almost $17,000.

Appreciation is not the only benefit to Murphy. Each month

that Murphy pays his mortgage, his debt to the lender decreases, a process known as *amortization*.

When mortgages are first created, little debt is paid off each month. In our example, Murphy's mortgage costs $800 per month, of which $765.63 represents interest and just $34.78 is used to pay principal in the first month. In two years, despite payments worth more than $20,000, Murphy will reduce his debt by only $924.23.

Murphy's equity after two years is not enough to allow retirement or to vault him into the ranks of the landed gentry. But since Murphy and his wife together make $42,000 a year, over a two-year period they will generate income worth $84,000. The equity built up in their house amounts to a silent savings rate equal to nearly 20 percent of their total pretax income.

We can also look at the equity gained by Murphy somewhat differently. We said his property value rose 7 percent a year, but Murphy didn't pay $97,250 for his home. He paid $12,000 in cash.

Murphy has to live somewhere, so we can say his monthly costs represent an economic "rent" and that his actual investment was the cash used to acquire his property. After two years, Murphy's property is worth $111,341 compared with the original $97,250 purchase price—a difference of $14,091. He invested $12,000 in cash up front, so he has a compounded annual return of 47.45 percent.

Murphy's return rate sounds wonderful, but prospective purchasers should understand that while a larger equity increases Murphy's net worth, his rate of return is a pleasant fiction. To capture his equity, Murphy must either sell or refinance. If he sells, he may face substantial marketing expenses, say 6 to 8 percent of the property's total value. If he refinances, a lender will only allow Murphy to borrow 75 to 85 percent of the property's entire value. In either case, Murphy's apparent equity is not available.

If Murphy holds on to his property, and if values continue to rise, he will begin to accumulate substantial equity. After five years his mortgage balance will drop to $84,771.24, and if values continue to increase 7 percent annually, in five years the property will be worth $136,398.16 and his equity will exceed $50,000. (See Table 4.)

Table 4   MURPHY'S EQUITY BUILD-UP

	Market Value	Mortgage Balance	Equity
	Purchase Price: $97,250		
	Annual Appreciation: 7 Percent		
Year 1	$104,057.50	$87,062.02	$16,995.48
Year 2	$111,341.53	$86,575.77	$24,765.76
Year 3	$119,135.44	$86,035.94	$33,099.50
Year 4	$127,474.92	$85,436.62	$42,038.30
Year 5	$136,398.16	$84,771.24	$51,626.92

As for Clark, since he is not an owner, he will not share the profits if property values rise. And since Clark is not responsible for the mortgage, such amortization as may accrue belongs to the owner.

In considering possible appreciation, prospective buyers should proceed with a strong dose of reality. *Not every property goes up, and the fact that values have risen dramatically in the past does not guarantee future profits.*

OTHER TAX BENEFITS

Write-offs for mortgage interest and property taxes, plus the ability to itemize deductions, define current tax advantages that real estate owners enjoy. In addition, there are long-term benefits that should not be overlooked.

If you buy stock at $14 a share and sell at $18, there is a tax on the $4 profit. No one cares if the money is invested in more stock, in stock with a higher purchase price, or if the money is used to finance a trip to Hong Kong.

With a *personal residence,* the rules today are different. If you buy a home for $100,000 and sell for $125,000, there is a $25,000 profit. If you then buy a prime residence of equal or greater value, the tax is deferred under what is known as the rollover residence replacement rule.

In addition to deferring taxes, the rollover rule is attractive because it talks about housing prices, not how profits must be used. With our example, we must buy a home worth at least $125,000, but we are not obligated to actually invest our $25,000 profit in a new home. If we can find a $125,000 property and finance the deal with loans worth $125,000, no one will ask how we used the $25,000 profit from the first house.

In the process of "reforming taxes" in 1986 and to a lesser extent each year thereafter, there has been a pronounced effort to first reduce and then eliminate consumer interest deductions. Home interest deductions are a notable exception, an exception that raises the question: Just how much can you borrow on your home with the blessings of Uncle Sam?

In general terms, interest on funds borrowed to acquire, build, or significantly improve a home are deductible up to $1,000,000, a ceiling which should not hamper most first-time buyers or anyone else. Owners may also use their home as security and borrow up to $100,000 in addition to basic acquisition and improvement costs.

The extra $100,000 is especially important because it means owners can use their homes to borrow money and still qualify for interest write-offs. For example, if you need $15,000 to purchase an automobile and secure financing with the car, the interest is regarded as consumer debt. If you have a home equity loan and borrow $15,000, the interest is fully deductible.

One reason home prices have risen over time is not so much that homes have become more valuable, but instead that the buying power of cash has declined. To provide for those age 55 and over who want to sell their homes and move to less expensive housing or a rental unit, the government has a special rule. If you sell a personal residence that you have lived in for three of the past five years, and if you are age 55 or older, then you have a one-time opportunity to shield as much as $125,000 in profits from federal taxes.

Still another tax benefit from Uncle Sam takes place at closing. If you pay points (loan discount fees) to acquire a personal residence, then such points are generally deductible in the year paid. Points paid to acquire investment property or to refinance can only be deducted over the entire loan term, typically 15 to 30 years.

We live in a society where computers, fax machines, and

modems make home offices increasingly practical, especially as an alternative to lengthy commutes downtown. Many people have home offices and claim proportional deductions for mortgage interest, property taxes, insurance, utilities, and related expenses. For example, if 10 percent of your home is used as an office, then 10 percent of mortgage interest costs, property taxes, and other expenses can be deducted. Also, space used for commercial purposes can be depreciated, a write-off not usually available to homeowners.

In addition to homeowners, renters with home offices may also be entitled to certain deductions, one of the few instances where renters get a tax break. While an office space write-off for depreciation is not available to renters, they may be able to claim a portion of their rent as a business expense.

For the latest rules, regulations, forms, exceptions, qualifications, details, and interpretations, speak with a knowledgeable CPA or tax attorney for advice concerning your specific situation.

PERSONAL SATISFACTION

So far we have concentrated on the financial issues that separate owners from renters, but many prospective purchasers want personal real estate because homes reflect our social standing and financial success; they are a standard by which others judge us.

We live in a society where each day presents its measures. We gauge our performance on the job or in school. We watch our friends, neighbors, and relatives, check their progress, and see how we compare.

We total out bank account, grateful for "overdraft protection," a euphemism that allows us to spend more than we save, and sometimes more than we earn. And our wallets bulge with credit cards so that even if we can't keep up with the Joneses, at least we can consume like they do.

But only some measures are economic. We know there are senses that feel good, that status and ego are important, and that money is not a substitute for health, happiness, companionship, or emotional security.

Somewhere in this constant process of assessment and achievement is a home, a measure of accomplishment but also a nest, a bastion in a hostile world, and much more.

Thus the urge to buy a first home includes more than favorable tax rules or possible appreciation. A home reflects who we are, what we have achieved, and how we want the world to see us. These values are not readily computed on a chart or marked on a graph, but they are surely important.

4

How Much Can You Borrow?

If there's one subject that seems to hold a universal attraction it's money, specifically someone else's. How can one otherwise explain the ongoing fascination with the monetary affairs of the wealthy, the famous, and the infamous?

Unlike the rich, first-time homebuyers rarely face a financial surplus. Money is tough to earn and hard to save, but without it homebuying is implausible.

Trying to determine buying ability is not an easy matter. We can look through a lender's eyes and find one result, or we can consider tax implications and obtain a different view. The cash we have available will influence our decision, as will our future income prospects.

Personal choices are also important. A willingness to save and sacrifice, to avoid credit card debt, to put off the purchase of a new car, to live with less than we can afford—such decisions may spell the difference between homeownership and renting.

FRONT AND BACK RATIOS

The Mortons were driving out to visit friends one day when they saw an open house and decided to stop. It was an enchanting house with a big lot. The place needed repairs, but it was the type of work a couple could do at night and on weekends. The broker, Mr. Taylor, explained that he worked for the sellers and would be happy to answer any questions.

The Mortons were not house hunting when they started their drive, but here was a perfect property. The location was good, the size was right, and the price tag was within the realm of affordability. The Mortons decided to make an offer.

"You're asking $150,000 for this place," said Mr. Morton. "We like it but it needs repairs and we're concerned about how much it will cost to fix up. We can offer $130,000."

"I can only tell you," said Taylor, "that the owners will accept $150,000. I don't know if they'll take $130,000, but if you make a written offer I'm obligated to submit it. I work for the owners and if you offer $130,000, I will suggest that they continue marketing the property because I think they can do better."

The Mortons and Taylor sat at the dining room table for over an hour discussing the property. After talking back and forth, the Mortons offered $140,000.

"With your offer," said broker Taylor, "we'll need a financial profile, something that tells us about your income and assets. We like you, but this is a business matter and your offer is no better than your ability to finance the deal. If we don't know about your finances, we could be in a situation where the property is under contract and the contract falls through. You would get your deposit back, but we will lose valuable time and opportunities while the property is off the market. In addition, it's the sellers who will continue to pay taxes, utility costs, and mortgage bills while the property remains unsold."

Everything Taylor said was true and reasonable. He was representing his clients and he was protecting them as well.

"Look," said Mr. Morton, "let's go through the numbers together and see if a workable deal is possible. Between us we make $55,000 a year and we have enough cash to cover a 10 percent down payment plus closing costs."

As for debts, the Mortons paid just $125 a month for an old school loan, $450 a month for auto financing on two small cars, and $40 each month for required credit card payments. In total: $615 a month—not much in the context of their income.

That broker Taylor wanted financial information from the Mortons is hardly unique. Smart brokers and sellers around the country realize that for purchase offers to have value, buyers must be able to obtain financing. In turn, to estimate how much one can afford, the issue of *ratios* must be considered.

Every lender has guidelines to determine whether or not loan applicants qualify for mortgages, and at the heart of such guidelines are ratios.

Front ratios concern the amount of income lenders allow borrowers to employ to pay basic housing costs. The central expenses here include mortgage principal, mortgage interest, real estate taxes, and property insurance, what is known by industry insiders as PITI.

PITI works well for single-family homes, but for those who buy condominiums, cooperatives, and private unit developments, there are additional costs lenders commonly include with PITI such as monthly fees, dues, and assessments owners must pay.

Suppose, for example, a single-family home and a condominium each cost $100,000. Assume also that there is a $75 monthly condo fee. Even though the two properties are priced alike, the condo buyer will need more income to qualify for a loan. Or, viewed from a different perspective, buyers can pay more for a single-family home than for a condo.

Since such items as condo fees and homeowner dues may not be any greater than the maintenance costs for a single-family home, why do lenders include such costs when figuring front ratios? Because fees, assessments, and dues may be liens against the property, bills that if left unpaid can result in foreclosure.

Back ratios include PITI plus all the regular monthly expenses faced by a prospective purchaser, items such as car loans, credit card payments, student loans, alimony, child support and judgments.

LOAN-TO-VALUE RATIOS (LTVs)

Knowing what front and back ratios include, we can now examine how they are used. Suppose the Mortons want a deal with 10 percent down, what lenders call a "90 percent LTV loan" or "90 percent financing."

With 90 percent financing the amount borrowed is equal to 90 percent of the purchase price. For the Mortons to buy property with a 90 percent LTV loan, they will need a $14,000 down payment and a $126,000 loan. They will also need additional cash for taxes, legal fees, a survey, termite inspection, and other services required to close the deal.

We know that the Mortons want 90 percent financing, but now we must consider the lender's viewpoint. Lenders may be willing to make 90 percent loans, but each may employ different qualification guidelines. For instance, First Federal uses 28/36 ratios, Second Federal uses 35/42, and Third Federal uses 45/45.

If the Mortons borrow $126,000 at 10.5 percent interest, monthly payments for principal and interest will total $1,152. PITI includes not only principal and interest, but taxes and insurance as well. Let's say that taxes are $1,020 a year and insurance costs $350.

So now we have our front ratio costs: Principal and interest equal $1,152, taxes are $85 per month ($1,020 divided by 12) and insurance is $29 ($350 divided by 12)—a total of $1,266 for PITI. (See Table 5.)

The Mortons earn $55,000 a year before deductions. If we take $55,000 and divide that figure by 12, the gross monthly income is $4,583. In this case, the projected PITI ($1,266) is equal to 27.62 percent of the Morton's gross monthly income. This same figure, 27.62 percent, is also their front ratio.

What about the back ratio? If we take PITI costs ($1,266) and add monthly costs for car payments ($450), student loans ($125), and minimum credit card payments ($40), we have monthly obligations of $1,881. With a total monthly income of $4,583, the

Table 5   PITI AND THE MORTONS

Down Payment	$14,000
Loan Amount	$126,000
Interest Rate	10.5 percent
Principal and Interest	$1,152
Taxes	$85
Insurance	$29
Total	$1,266

Mortons' back ratio is 41.04 percent ($1,881 divided by $4,583).

We can now see that the Mortons have a front ratio of 27.62 and a back ratio of 41.04, not good enough to qualify with First Federal but okay under the guidelines employed by Second Federal and Third Federal. (See Table 6.)

The Mortons were lucky to find lenders willing to make 90 percent loans *and* to allow ratios greater than 28/36. *In most cases, lenders who offer 90 percent, fixed-rate financing will stick closely to 28/36 ratios.*

What would happen if no financing was available to the Mortons except with 28/36 ratios? Without changing one or more conditions, the Mortons will not be able to buy their dream house. However, the deal might work if:

- Instead of borrowing $126,000 from a lender, the Mortons borrow from the sellers. But few sellers can provide enough financing to eliminate the need for a lender; most sellers want cash from the sale to buy a new home.

- The sellers lower their price. If the monthly payments for principal and interest are reduced by $252.16 from $1,152.57 to $900.41, then the Mortons can borrow $98,433.51. If the amount borrowed by the Mortons equals 90 percent of the purchase price, the sellers would then have to accept $109,370

Table 6   WHAT THE MORTONS CAN AFFORD

Annual Income	$55,000
Monthly Income	$4,583
Monthly Payments	
Car Loans (2)	$450
Student Loan	$125
Required Credit Card Payments	$40
Total Monthly Payments	$615
PITI	$1,266
PITI Plus Expenses	$1,881
Front Ratio	27.62 percent
Back Ratio	41.04 percent

for their property. Note that closing costs and insurance payments may also decline if the sellers accept a markedly lower price.

- Interest rates are lower. Rather than interest at 10.5 percent, if the qualifying interest rate is 7.73 percent, the Mortons will have initial monthly payments of $900.94. Such financing may be available with graduated payment loans, or GPMs, a form of financing where rates can start 4 to 5 percent below fixed-rate loans.

- The loan term is longer. Instead of a 30-year mortgage, why not a 40-year loan? If the loan term is extended by 10 years, monthly costs will drop to $1,119.60—a $32.97 reduction, but not nearly enough to make the deal work.

- The Mortons pay off some of their consumer debts. Buyers should be aware that lender policies in this area vary. Some lenders will *not* accept payoffs. That is, if you owe $1,000 on a credit card and are required to pay $40 each month, if you pay off the bill at the time you apply for financing or even just before, lenders may continue to count the $40 as a monthly expense. The reason is that with revolving credit lines, a debt that is paid off today can be quickly replaced with new debt tomorrow.

In contrast, lenders may elect not to count monthly debts when few payments remain. If you have two car payments left, some lenders will not regard the payments as a monthly expense. *Before paying off debts, always ask about lender policies.*

What happens if the Mortons want the property but the sellers won't lower their price or take back financing? What happens if lower interest rates and other remedies are not available? Add more cash and the deal becomes entirely plausible.

MORE CASH, BETTER TERMS

When we first mentioned ratios, we said lenders often require 28/36 ratios for those who pay down 10 percent. Left unstated was another consideration: Most lenders have guidelines that depend on the type of loan being sought (fixed-rate or adjustable, for example) and the amount paid up front by the purchasers. As down payments become larger, ratios become more liberal. For instance, with 20 percent down, ratios of 33/38 rather than 28/36 may be available from First Federal.

Lenders have more liberal guidelines for larger down payments because they have less risk. If the Mortons put down 10 percent and the lender needs to foreclose, there's only $14,000 between the loan amount and the property's sale value. If the Mortons put down 20 percent, $28,000 in this case, the lender will be much happier, a happiness reflected in more liberal ratios.

With a larger down payment, the Mortons' deal looks like this: First, they put down $28,000.

Second, instead of a $126,000 mortgage, they only borrow $112,000.

Third, the interest rate may be lower because the loan represents less risk to the lender.

Fourth, not only can the interest rate fall when the Mortons put down 20 percent, up-front charges also drop. As an example, a lender may require the payment of one *point* at settlement. One point is equal to 1 percent of the loan amount. If the Mortons put down 10 percent and borrow $126,000, one point will equal $1,260. If they put down 20 percent, one point will equal $1,120 (1 percent of $112,000).

Fifth, taxes ($85 per month) and insurance ($29 per month) remain the same. If we combine these costs with lower monthly mortgage expenses ($1,025), then the PITI for this loan is $1,139 and the front ratio is a comfortable 24.85 ($1,139 divided by $4,583).

Sixth, the back ratio is now equal to the PITI ($1,139) plus monthly costs for auto loans ($450), student financing ($125), and credit card bills ($40), a $1,754 total, or a back ratio of 38.27 ($1,754 divided by $4,583). (See Table 7.)

What our example clearly shows is that by placing more money down, monthly payments are reduced and therefore many people will find that housing is substantially more affordable. The problem, of course, is that few first-time buyers have enough cash to make large down payments.

Table 7   THE MORTONS' PURCHASE WITH 10 PERCENT AND
20 PERCENT DOWN

	10 percent	*20 percent*
Purchase Price	$140,000	$140,000
Down Payment	$14,000	$28,000
Loan Amount	$126,000	$112,000
Interest Rate	10.5 percent	10.5 percent
1 Point	$1,260	$1,120
Monthly Payment	$1,152	$1,025
Taxes	$85	$85
Insurance	$29	$29
PITI	$1,266	$1,139
Monthly Expenses	$615	$615
Front Ratio	27.62 percent	24.85 percent
Back Ratio	41.04 percent	38.27 percent

WHAT'S YOUR BORROWING POWER?

We saw that the Mortons used the "love at first sight" homebuying method, an approach long on romance but often short on
results.

The Mortons found a property and then attempted to figure
out what they could afford. We can also approach financing from
the other direction. Given income and debts, we can determine
how much financing might be available on a conservative basis
with a simple chart and the use of a pencil, calculator, or personal
computer to figure the results. (See Table 8.)

Step One.   Add your total annual income. By *income* lenders
mean an average of your earnings over the past two years *before*
taxes—salary, self-employment income, interest, dividends, etc.
If you receive alimony, child support, or separate maintenance
you may elect to count such payments as income, or you may
decide not to disclose them. Since you want the ability to borrow
as much as possible it makes sense to detail such payments on a
loan application. Divide your annual income into a monthly average.

Buy Your First Home Now

Table 8   HOW MUCH CAN YOU AFFORD?

Annual Income	$_____
Monthly Income	$_____ (1)

Projected Monthly Mortgage Payment	$_____
Taxes	$_____
Insurance	$_____
Total PITI	$_____ (2)
Front Ratio = (2) Divided By (1)	
Front Ratio = _____ Percent	

Monthly Payments

Car Loan	$_____
Student Loan	$_____
Required Credit Card Payments	
Card #1	$_____
Card #2	$_____
Card #3	$_____
Monthly Expenses	$_____
Monthly Expenses + PITI = $_____ (3)	
Back Ratio = (3) Divided By (1)	
Back Ratio = _____ Percent	

Step Two.   Speak with brokers and loan officers to estimate monthly costs for principal and interest. Table 9 shows how monthly expenses for principal and interest vary according to the amount borrowed and the rate of interest. A financial calculator or personal computer with appropriate software can provide more precise figures.

Step Three.   Speak with brokers, loan officers, and property owners to determine area property taxes. If you buy a home for $100,000, $125,000, or $150,000, how much should you expect to pay for taxes *each month?*

Step Four.   Speak to brokers, owners, and insurance agents to determine how much property insurance will cost each month

Table 9 BASIC 30-YEAR MORTGAGE CHART: MONTHLY COSTS FOR PRINCIPAL AND INTEREST

	8.5	9.0	9.5	10.00	10.5
$50,000	$384.46	$402.31	$420.43	$438.79	$457.37
$55,000	$422.90	$442.54	$462.47	$482.66	$503.11
$60,000	$461.35	$482.77	$504.51	$526.54	$548.84
$65,000	$499.79	$523.00	$546.56	$570.42	$594.58
$70,000	$538.24	$563.24	$588.60	$614.30	$640.32
$75,000	$576.69	$603.47	$630.64	$658.18	$686.05
$80,000	$615.13	$643.70	$672.68	$702.06	$731.79
$85,000	$653.58	$683.93	$714.73	$745.94	$777.53
$90,000	$692.02	$724.16	$756.77	$789.81	$823.27
$95,000	$730.47	$764.39	$798.81	$833.69	$869.00
$100,000	$768.91	$804.62	$840.85	$877.57	$914.74

for homes valued at $100,000, $125,000, $150,000, or whatever figure might be appropriate.

Step Five. Combine monthly costs for principal, interest, taxes, and insurance. Divide this total by your monthly income. This is your front ratio.

Step Six. List your monthly debts for such expenses as car payments, loans, required credit card payments, etc. Add these debts.

Step Seven. Combine your monthly debts with PITI. Take this total amount and divide by your monthly income. This is your back ratio.

The guidelines above provide a *general* idea of your ability to finance real estate. But because all individuals have unique financial considerations, and because lender guidelines vary from company to company and from loan product to loan product, it is important to speak with individual loan officers to calculate your actual borrowing ability.

QUOTED RATES VERSUS QUALIFYING RATES

To this point, we have seen that affordability is determined in part by quoted interest rates. With the Mortons, we estimated their borrowing ability in a market where lenders wanted 10.5 percent interest for fixed-rate financing.

First-time buyers should be aware, however, that quoted rates are not always appropriate when figuring how much you can borrow.

With fixed-rate loans, the interest rate will be the same during the entire mortgage term and therefore it is the rate that can be used to estimate borrowing power.

With *adjustable rate mortgages,* or ARMs, the story is different. ARMs typically have low start rates—so-called "teaser" rates—which then rise over time.

Although some lenders *do* qualify borrowers on the basis of ARM start rates, most use a different system.

To qualify for ARM financing, some lenders look not at the initial start rate, but at the *highest rate possible in the second year.* As an example, if an ARM has a 8 percent start rate and the interest rate can rise by a maximum of 2 percent yearly, then the highest rate in the loan's second year would be 10 percent.

Another approach lenders frequently use is to take the start rate and add 1 percent. For an ARM with an 8 percent start rate, the qualifying rate would be 9 percent.

POINTS AND PRICING

Loans are often hard to compare, sometimes because descriptions are vague and at other times because it can be difficult to match different combinations of rates and points.

A "1-year" ARM to some lenders is an ARM where the interest rates and monthly payments remain the same for 12 months. Another lender may view a "1-year" ARM as a loan where monthly payments remain the same, but monthly interest costs vary.

To make matters more complex, we live in a world where one "10 percent" mortgage may have a higher interest rate than another "10 percent" mortgage. The difference between them is money paid at closing, what lenders call *loan discount fees* or points.

A point, as mentioned earlier, is equal to 1 percent of the initial loan amount. Borrow $100,000 from a lender, and one point at closing will cost $1,000.

Consider what happens when a point is paid. With a $100,000 loan, the lender receives $1,000 at settlement, which means the borrower can only use $99,000. Unfortunately the full $100,000 is still owed to the lender.

So now we have a situation where the borrower owes $100,000, pays interest on $100,000, but gives $1,000 to the lender at closing. If the lender charges 10 percent interest, the true interest rate over 30 years is 10.12 percent. Why? Because less than $100,000 is outstanding. (See Table 10.)

A point equals roughly one-eighth of a percent over 30 years. Since most loans only last one-third that long, a point is worth far more to lenders. If we translate points into interest rates, then a loan priced at 10 percent plus 2 points has a 30-year rate equal to approximately 10.25 percent.

At any time we can find many loan rates as we shop for financing—10 percent plus 2 points, 10.25 percent plus 1 point, etc. For such quotes to make sense, and to make reasonable rate comparisons, we must translate rate-and-point combinations into simple rates. For example, 10 percent plus 2 points is equal to 10.25 percent over 30 years. A loan at 10.25 percent plus 1 point is equal to 10.375 percent over 30 years.

Whether it's better to pay more points or lower rates, or fewer points and higher rates, is more complex.

Suppose you can choose between two $100,000 loans, one at 10.5 percent plus 2 points and the other at 11 percent and no points. Which do you choose?

Table 10   THE TRUE COST OF POINTS

Amount Borrowed	$100,000
Less 1 Point	$1,000
Amount Received	$99,000
Apparent Interest Rate	10.0000 percent
True Interest Rate	10.1198 percent

Table 11   COMPARING LOANS AND POINTS

Loan Amount	$100,000	$100,000
Face Rate	10.50 percent	11 percent
Points	2	0
Settlement Cost For Points	$2,000	0
Monthly Payment	$914.74	$952.32
Extra Monthly Cost	0	$37.58
True Interest Rate	10.75 percent	11 percent

The loan with 2 points will cost $2,000 at settlement, and the monthly payment for principal and interest over 30 years will amount to $914.74.

The 11 percent loan has no up-front cost for points, but the monthly expense is $952.32.

The first loan costs $2,000 more at settlement but the 11 percent mortgage costs an additional $37.60 per month. Divide $2,000 by $37.60 and it will take roughly 54 months of ownership before the 11 percent loan is more expensive. (See Table 11.)

For first-time buyers, the better loan choice is the 10.5 percent mortgage with two points—if your intent is to own the property for more than 54 months. If a property is being purchased with short-term ownership in mind, then the 11 percent loan—the loan with a higher interest rate—is the better deal.

As a practical matter, paying money for points at settlement may not be an option for cash-pressed first-time buyers. Paying higher interest rates is not attractive either since higher rates mean more costly monthly payments and thus less ability to qualify for a loan.

The best choice, by far, works like this: Try to have the seller pay some or all of the points. If the marketplace is sufficiently flooded with homes for sale, if interest rates are rising, paying points may well be attractive to sellers.

5

Cash, Down Payments, and Alternatives

In Chapter 4 we saw that it was possible to determine *borrowing* capacity based on income and debts. But income and debts rarely define how much housing we can afford. In addition to a loan, we need cash.

Cash is important for a simple reason: No traditional lender, except with insurance from the Veterans Administration, will provide 100 percent financing.

Thus we find a curious problem. Many people have good incomes and can afford monthly mortgage payments, but they lack savings and therefore the ability to make a down payment from their own resources.

From the lender's perspective it's easy to understand why a cash commitment—equity—is important.

Imagine a deal where Wiggins buys a home for $100,000 and receives a $100,000 loan from First National. A few months later Wiggins moves to the Malay Peninsula, leaving behind both his home and an unpaid mortgage.

Even if First National promptly forecloses, it will lose money on the deal. Foreclosure expenses, coupled with lost interest payments, makes the loan to Wiggins a terrible deal.

But it's doubtful that Wiggins would have left so quickly if his money was tied up in the property. If he had put down $10,000, $20,000, or more, you can bet that he would have taken the time to sell the property and repay the lender before venturing overseas.

Deals with little or no money down are risky for lenders, and lenders do not like excess risk. What lenders want, what they demand, and what they usually get is either cash from the buyer up front or solid guarantees from a third party to assure the loan's repayment.

THE CASH CRUNCH

If there's an endangered species in this country, it's the individual or couple who actually save money. Cash is not only in limited supply, each day brings new efforts to separate people from their money.

We have seasonal fashions, new car introductions, shopping plazas, anniversary sales, and holiday mark-downs. And while nothing is wrong with spending money for needed items, for would-be homebuyers the definition of *needed* excludes many frills and fashions.

Would-be buyers routinely cannot afford a first house because so much of their capital has been routed to other purchases. New cars are wonderful, but they represent large monthly costs and thus less ability to qualify for a loan. The latest fashion may be chic and in style, but money spent for this year's hottest outfits is money not saved.

The simple reality is that first-time buyers must save money. Forget a new car, the trip to Rio, an expensive wardrobe, credit cards, new appliances, weekly visits to trendy restaurants, or any expense not absolutely necessary.

Instead, begin a campaign to save money. Now.

There are three steps that can produce immediate results.

First, open a savings account or money market fund, something that pays interest, protects your principal, allows immediate access to your money, and does not charge ridiculous fees to open an account, to leave an account, to maintain an account, or to withdraw money.

Second, set up a budget and find out where your money goes. See what you spend each week and where expenses can be cut. Even small savings, $5 here or $10 there, can add up.

Third, consider that whatever you make today, other people earn less. At least for the short term, construct a lifestyle that reflects a smaller income, fewer expenditures, and more savings.

CONVENTIONAL FINANCING

The most basic home mortgage is the plain and simple conventional loan where the buyer puts down a cash amount equal to 20 percent of the purchase price and a lender provides a loan for the balance.

In addition to a 20 percent down payment, conventional loans are distinguished by several features.

- The loan's term is typically 30 years.

- There is one interest rate throughout the entire loan term.

- Monthly payments remain unchanged throughout the loan term.

- The entire debt is paid off when the loan term is finished.

As an example, if Berger buys a $100,000 property, he will put down 20 percent of the purchase price in cash, $20,000 in this case, and obtain a 30-year, $80,000 mortgage. If the interest rate is 10.5 percent, he will have payments for principal and interest of $731.79 monthly for 30 years. (See Table 12.)

Conventional loans offer stability because interest rates and monthly payment are established up front. Changing rates and confusing terms are not a problem.

Conventional loans are also attractive for another reason. The buying power of cash is eroded by inflation and the set monthly payments required with conventional financing represent less real cost over time.

Suppose that today $1 buys goods and services worth $1. Suppose also that the inflation rate is 6.7 percent. In ten years,

Table 12   MR. BERGER'S
CONVENTIONAL LOAN

Sale Price	$100,000
Down Payment	$20,000
Loan Amount	$80,000
Interest Rate	10.5 percent
Loan Term	30 years
Monthly Payment	$731.79

the buying power of $1 will be chopped in half. If you have $750 mortgage payments today, then ten years from now your real mortgage cost measured in today's buying power will be just $375.

While declining real costs are good news for borrowers, lenders are not so happy. It's their money that buys less and less each year.

For first-time borrowers, the issues surrounding conventional loans are both interesting and moot. Yes, a fixed-rate loan is attractive, but who among us has 20 percent to put down? Take that large down payment, add hefty closing costs, and borrowers thinking about conventional financing for $100,000 properties, homes at the bottom of the market in many areas, will need $22,000 to $25,000 up front, not counting moving costs, decorating, painting, carpets, and repairs.

15-YEAR LOANS

Conventional financing offers many benefits for those who have substantial savings, but one major problem with 30-year loans is the massive interest bill they represent.

If you borrow $100,000 at 10.5 percent interest, the monthly payments will total $914.74. Over 30 years there will be 360 equal payments, or a total bill for $329,306.40 ($914.74 × 360). Of this amount, $100,000 is principal and the balance—$229,306—is interest.

The interest bill is steep because the loan is outstanding for many years. If you borrow for a shorter period, interest costs fall substantially.

If we use the same principal amount ($100,000) and the same interest rate (10.5 percent), we can see what happens if the loan term is shortened.

- With a 25-year term, the monthly cost rises to $944.18. The potential interest bill drops to $183,254.51.

- With a 20-year loan, the monthly payment goes up to $998.38. If held for 20 years, the interest cost will total $139,611.17.

- With a 15-year loan, monthly payments of $1,105.40 will be required. Total potential interest: Just $98,971.81, or $130,334.19 less than a 30-year mortgage. (See Table 13.)

It should be said that our example understates the savings 15-year loans offer. In many cases, interest rates for 15-year financing are priced .25 to .50 percent lower than 30-year loans because mortgages with shorter terms represent less risk to lenders.

With shorter terms, monthly costs rise and total interest charges fall. This is good news for those who can afford higher monthly payments, an option not shared by many first-time buyers.

Not only are first-time buyers unlikely to afford the higher monthly payments required for 15-year financing, they are also unlikely to qualify for such loans in the first place. Because mortgages with shorter terms have higher monthly payments, they require more income to qualify for financing.

PREPAYMENTS

Shorter loans can be created in two ways. Many lenders make 15-, 20-, and 25-year loans, mortgages which from the beginning offer important economies. Another approach is to obtain a full-term, 30-year mortgage and voluntarily make larger payments than the lender requires, either monthly or from time to time.

The problem with prepayments, however, is that many lenders—especially those who make fixed-rate loans—frown on them.

Table 13   15- AND 30-YEAR FINANCING COMPARED

Loan Amount	$100,000	$100,000
Loan Term	30 years	15 years
Interest Rate	10.5 percent	10.5 percent*
Monthly Payment	$914.74	$1,105.40
Potential Interest Bill	$229,306	$98,972
Potential Interest Savings	0	$130,334

*Actual 15-year interest rates are often less than 30-year rates.

Some more than frown, they charge a prepayment penalty.

Prepayments without penalty can be made on FHA, VA, and many older conventional loans—those established before 1980. Prepayments without penalty can also be made on most adjustable rate mortgages.

Although prepayments shorten loan terms for fixed-rate financing, their effect on ARMs is somewhat different.

With a typical ARM, the interest rate and monthly payments are adjusted regularly, say every 6 or 12 months. If a borrower makes prepayments, the loan balance declines more rapidly than would otherwise be possible. The result is that at the time payments are recalculated there is less debt on which interest may be charged.

With less debt, monthly payments should go down—*but only if interest rates remain steady or fall.* If ARM interest rates rise, monthly *payments* can actually increase even though the principal balance has declined.

Suppose $100,000 is outstanding and the interest rate is 10 percent. The monthly payment will be $877.57. In the second year, suppose the principal balance has been reduced to $97,000. If the interest rate remains at 10 percent, the monthly payment will drop to $856. If the interest rate rises to 11 percent, then $927.93 will be due each month—even though the principal balance has been reduced. (See Table 14.)

Bi-weekly mortgages are formalized prepayment plans, although they are not usually described this way. With a bi-weekly loan, borrowers make payments every two weeks. In rough terms, the payments are equal to half the amount that monthly payments require, perhaps $500 rather than $1,000. The result is that the loan is paid off early, usually in 18 to 20 years. (See Table 15.)

Table 14 ARM RATES AND PAYMENTS

Principal Amount	$100,000	$97,000
Interest Rate	10 percent	11 percent
Monthly Payment	$877.57	$927.93
Principal Decline	0	$3,000.00
Payment Increase	0	$50.36

Table 15   CONVENTIONAL VERSUS BI-WEEKLY LOANS

Loan Amount	$100,000	$100,000
Interest Rate	10.5 percent	10.5 percent
Payments Per Year	12	26
Payment Size	$914.74	$457.37
Potential Loan Term	30 years	20.45 years
Potential Interest Cost	$229,306	$143,460
Potential Interest Savings	0	$85,846

For example, a 30-year loan for $100,000 requires monthly payments of $914.74. Under a bi-weekly plan, a payment of $422.05 would be required for a 30-year loan. If we raise the payment to $457.37—half the regular monthly cost—then the loan can be repaid in 20.45 years and the interest bill can be reduced by $85,845.68 (the bi-weekly interest cost equals $143,460.47 while a 30-year loan with monthly payments has an interest cost of $229,306.15).

How does a bi-weekly loan cut interest costs? With conventional loans, borrowers make 12 monthly payments. With bi-weekly financing, borrowers make payments every two weeks, 26 payments a year, or the equivalent of 13 monthly payments.

Given a choice between loans where there is a right to prepay without penalty or a bi-weekly payment schedule, first-time buyers should opt for the right to prepay without penalty. As your income goes up you can always make additional payments. If your income goes down or you are beset by temporary financial problems, you will not be bound to the rigors and costs of a bi-weekly payment schedule.

FHA LOANS

For most first-time buyers, conventional financing resembles a fleet of yachts, something that can be described but not attained. It doesn't matter whether one is or is not attracted by conventional loans, whether they have a 30-year term or run for 15 years, or whether you have any interest in prepaying such financing. The fact is that with a 20 percent down payment, conventional loans are not a reasonable financial choice for most first-time buyers.

But loans that largely resemble conventional financing are available, loans that feature 30-year terms, equal monthly payments, and set interest rates. These very same loans also feature down payments below 5 percent!

Commonly known as FHA financing, such loans are available everywhere under what is called the 203(b) program. They work like this:

- The Federal Housing Administration (FHA) *insures* lenders in the event borrowers default. Thus FHA "loans" represent insured financing, not money from the federal treasury.

- With FHA backing, lenders will accept down payments on the following basis: 3 percent of the first $25,000, plus 5 percent of the balance. Buy a home for $100,000 with conventional financing and you will need $20,000 at closing. Buy under the FHA program, and the down payment totals just $4,500.

- FHA loans can be either fixed-rate or adjustable.

- FHA loans may be prepaid in whole or in part without penalty.

- FHA rates are set in the marketplace, just like conventional loans.

While FHA loans are exceedingly attractive when compared with conventional financing, they do raise several concerns.

First, the amount you can borrow is limited. Since first-time buyers are likely to purchase homes at entry-level prices, this is less of a problem than other buyers may face.

The general loan limitations for *owner-occupied* housing depend on whether you live in a "high cost" area or not. As this is written, FHA financing for as much as $124,875 is available for single-family homes, $140,600 for duplexes, $170,200 for triplexes, and $197,950 for four-unit properties. Even these loan limits may be higher in such locations as Alaska, Guam, and Hawaii. Check with local lenders for the latest loan limit figures.

Second, since FHA loans are backed by an insurance program, borrowers must pay insurance premiums.

Under the FHA formula, borrowers pay an insurance premium equal to 3.8 percent of the loan amount. Borrow $100,000 and the premium is $3,800.

The good news about this premium is that it can be financed. The insurance premium is simply added to the loan and paid off over time.

For a $90,000 mortgage at 10 percent interest, the monthly payment for principal and interest over 30 years will be $789.81, and the insurance premium will be $3,420. If $93,420 is borrowed with the same rates and terms, the monthly payment is $819.83, a $30.02 difference. For most people, it's far easier to come up with an extra $30 a month rather than $3,420 at closing. (See Table 16.)

Because the FHA insurance premium is paid up front, it may be possible to obtain a refund when you sell or refinance. For information, speak to your lender or call HUD at 202–755–5616.

Since the 1930s, almost 18 million FHA loans have been created, and of these, 6.5 million were outstanding when 1988 ended. In 1988, according to the National Association of Realtors, 72 percent of all FHA financing represented loans to first-time buyers, a percentage that confirms the singular importance of this program to entry-level purchasers.

Table 16 CONVENTIONAL VERSUS FHA FINANCING

	Conventional	*FHA*
Sale Price	$100,000	$100,000
Down Payment	$20,000	$10,000
Loan Amount	$80,000	$90,000
Mortgage Insurance	0	$3,420
Down Payment Plus Mortgage Insurance	$20,000	$13,420
Loan Term	30 years	30 years
Interest Rate	10.5 percent	10.5 percent
Monthly Payment	$731.79	$819.83

VA LOANS

While FHA insurance allows a borrower to obtain financing with less than 5 percent down, there is a federal program that offers an even better deal. With backing from the Veterans Administration, borrowers can obtain financing with no money down.

VA loans are available to those who have successfully completed their military service and to individuals who have served in certain other federal agencies, such as officers in the Public Health Service.

Like the FHA, the Veterans Administration does not make loans, it only guarantees their repayment. Such guarantees are now funded with a 1 percent charge at settlement, a fee that can be added to the loan so that no additional cost is incurred up front. (See Table 17.)

The way the VA program works, qualified individuals receive an "entitlement" that is currently set at $36,000. On loans up to $45,000, 50 percent of the principal is guaranteed. For loans above $45,000, the government insures 40 percent of the principal, but will not reimburse lenders more than $36,000.

In effect, there is no limit that prohibits lenders from making a $200,000 VA loan or an $800,000 mortgage, as long as the loan amount does not exceed the property's appraised value plus 1 percent.

As a practical matter, lenders are unlikely to make VA loans for more than $144,000. With a $144,000 loan and a $36,000

Table 17   CONVENTIONAL VERSUS VA FINANCING

	Conventional	VA
Sale Price	$100,000	$100,000
Down Payment	$20,000	0
Loan Amount	$80,000	$100,000
Mortgage Insurance	0	$1,000
Down Payment Plus Mortgage Insurance	$20,000	$1,000
Loan Term	30 years	30 years
Interest Rate	10.5 percent	10.5 percent
Monthly Payment	$731.79	$914.74

entitlement, lenders have the equivalent of financing with 25 percent down. If they made bigger loans under the VA program, the maximum entitlement would remain $36,000 but the level of protection would diminish. For example, with a $200,000 loan and a $36,000 entitlement, VA protection is equal to only 18 percent of the loan amount.

Although VA loans do not require down payments, such loans are rarely cash free. Buyers will need money for taxes, escrow accounts, and fees at closing.

Also, the benefit of 100 percent financing—no down payment—creates three significant drawbacks. First, if there is no down payment, the property must be financed with a large mortgage. Second, a large mortgage requires large monthly payments. Third, a large mortgage means steep interest costs because so much cash has been borrowed from a lender.

To obtain a VA loan, qualified first-time borrowers will need form DD 214, a certificate given upon release from military service, plus VA Form 26–1880, "Request for Certificate of Eligibility." When these two forms are presented at a local VA office, borrowers will then receive a "Certificate of Eligibility" which can be given to lenders.

If you qualify it makes sense to obtain needed VA forms and certificates before entering the housing market. For more information, contact your local VA office. You won't be the only first-time buyer asking questions. According to the National Association of Realtors, 64 percent of all VA loans issued in 1988 went to first-time purchasers.

PRIVATE MORTGAGE INSURANCE

As attractive as the FHA and VA programs may appear to those with limited capital, each plan has obvious limitations. Because FHA loan amounts are restricted, such financing may not be workable in high-cost urban and suburban areas. As for the VA program, it's simply out of reach to those without qualifying service.

The private sector has seen these limitations and filled the void with a product called *private mortgage insurance,* or PMI. Unlike "mortgage life insurance," which produces benefits when someone dies, mortgage insurance protects *lenders* when borrowers default.

Using PMI, a first-time buyer can obtain financing with 5, 10, or 15 percent down. If a borrower defaults, the lender's loan is protected in part by the insuror's promise to cover the loss. Between the buyer's down payment, private mortgage insurance, and the property's foreclosure value, lenders can make low-down-payment loans with little risk. (See Table 18.)

Since PMI is insurance, borrowers must pay premiums. How much borrowers pay for PMI coverage depends on the amount put down to acquire the property, the coverage amount required by the lender, and whether the loan has a fixed or adjustable rate. Here are typical PMI premiums charged at the time this book was developed.

- For borrowers who put down 5 percent for fixed-rate financing, the initial cost is 1 percent of the principal amount at settlement plus .50 percent each year. The .50 percent fee is divided by 12 and paid each month on the loan's outstanding principal balance.

- For borrowers who put down 10 percent for fixed-rate financing, the initial cost is .40 percent of the principal amount at settlement plus .35 percent each year.

- For borrowers who put down 15 percent for fixed-rate financing, the initial cost is .30 percent of the principal amount at settlement plus .30 percent each year.

Table 18   PMI VERSUS OTHER INSURANCE PROGRAMS

	PMI	FHA	VA
Loan Amount	$100,000	$100,000	$100,000
Premium	2.9 percent*	3.8 percent	1 percent
Cash Amount	$2,900	$3,800	$1,000
Refund Possible**	Yes	Yes	No
Payable Monthly	Yes	Yes	Yes

*PMI fee can vary according to loan coverage and down payment percentage.
**Refunds may be possible when FHA and PMI premiums are paid in a lump sum at closing.

- For borrowers who put down 5 percent for *adjustable-rate financing,* the initial cost is 1.20 percent of the principal amount at settlement plus .55 percent each year.

- For borrowers who put down 10 percent for adjustable-rate financing, the initial cost is .50 percent of the principal amount at settlement plus .45 percent each year.

- For borrowers who put down 15 percent for adjustable-rate financing, the initial cost is .35 percent of the principal amount at settlement plus .35 percent each year.

What do these numbers mean? If you borrow $100,000 with 10 percent down and fixed rates, you will pay $400 at closing plus approximately $350 for PMI during the loan's first year.

LUMP-SUM PMI

The figures above show that PMI can be paid with a small payment up front and then monthly payments over time. There is another approach to PMI, one that can reduce overall costs.

Rather than pay monthly PMI premiums, the entire PMI fee can be paid up front in a lump sum. For a $100,000, fixed-rate loan with 10 percent down, borrowers might expect to pay $2,950. Since first-time buyers are trying to reduce cash costs up front, a lump sum payment at closing may not seem attractive.

The trick is that a single payment doesn't have to be made at closing. Instead, the premium can be added to the loan amount and then paid back over time.

If you add $2,950 to the mortgage, you have more debt, more interest, and higher monthly payments. For a $2,950 principal increase with 10 percent financing, the additional monthly cost will be approximately $25.89. In comparison, annual PMI payments for a $100,000 loan can require $750 to be paid out the first year—$400 at settlement and roughly $350 over the first 12 months.

Also, since the lump-sum payment provides coverage over a given term, say 10 to 15 years, borrowers may be entitled to a rebate if the property is sold before coverage expires. Speak with lenders for specific details concerning PMI costs, the length of coverage provided, and the possibility of refunds.

The ability to obtain an eventual refund may seem enticing, but a better deal may be lump-sum PMI without a refund. Rather than $2,950 for a $100,000 fixed-rate loan with 10 percent down, the cost can drop to $2,200—an amount that can again be added to the loan and paid out over time.

Lori Stahl of Milwaukee's Mortgage Guarantee Insurance Corporation (MGIC), one of the nation's largest PMI companies, notes that lump-sum PMI is particularly attractive to purchasers who intend to occupy property for at least six or seven years. It is also far cheaper than the FHA insurance premium, a $3,800 expense for a $100,000 loan.

THE PARENT FACTOR

We saw in Chapter 1 that age is a major factor in the homebuying process. Many of those who are older and bought homes in past years have benefited from appreciation rates that have outstripped the cost of living.

Many of these very same folks who did so well over time are known to us as Mom and Dad. The homes they bought many years ago are now worth several times what they paid, and the interest costs for older loans, if such properties are encumbered with financing at all, carry prehistoric rates well below 10 percent.

That Mom and Dad have done well is good news, but will they share with the kids?

In some families gifts are easily given and parents are delighted to help their children. For those fortunate enough to have parents who are both financially successful and willing to share, homebuying can be greatly simplified.

Not only can parents make homebuying much easier for their children, such assistance is entirely common. A 1987 study by the National Association of Realtors shows that 16 percent of *all* homebuyers were aided by parents, *a figure that rose to 31 percent for first-time buyers.*

One approach to parental aid is an outright gift from Mom and Dad. Parents providing such funds are typically required by lenders to present a "gift letter" showing that the money is given freely and that all demands for repayment are waived. In addition, some lenders may also want to see account statements showing that the money is actually available for settlement.

Another approach to homebuying with parents works like this:

The Crowleys want to buy a new house for $100,000. Crowley the elder has a home worth $300,000, no mortgage, and a substantial income. Rather than finance the new house, the Crowley clan refinances the old one and buys the new property for cash.

The Crowleys can pay for their parental financing in several ways.

- Crowley senior can simply repay the entire loan, in effect giving the house as a gift. However, giving an entire house as a gift raises significant tax questions and may not be desirable.

- As an alternative to an outright grant, Crowley senior can give each younger Crowley $850 a month as a gift, a $10,000 annual total. The children can then use the gift money to cover Crowley senior's mortgage costs.

- In the morbid financing department, Crowley senior can carry life insurance with $100,000. If he dies, the younger Crowleys can pay off the $100,000 mortgage or pay part of it with nontaxable insurance proceeds. In effect, the insurance is a deferred gift. A twist has the insurance premiums paid by the children. Speak to an insurance broker for details and advice.

In considering a gift situation, parental lenders should be keenly aware that Uncle Sam will be interested in the tax issues such presents can create. Always consult with knowledgeable tax and estate professionals before making large gift commitments.

SELLER TAKE-BACKS

Another potential source of down payment money are would-be sellers. When sellers create loans that reduce down payment requirements, their homes are more salable.

One strategy might work like this: The buyer puts down 10

percent and the seller "takes back" (lends to the buyer) an amount equal to 10 percent of the purchase price. The balance of the money comes from a lender, who offers 80 percent financing.

If the house is being sold for $100,000, the seller will create a $10,000 loan. The seller will also receive $90,000 in cash for the property, $10,000 from the purchasers and $80,000 from a lender.

If take-backs are available buyers will need less cash. In addition, with 80 percent financing from a lender, private mortgage insurance may be unnecessary, therefore reducing up-front costs as well as monthly expenses.

A willingness (and an ability) to make a loan can also be attractive to sellers. In a market with high interest rates, seller financing might allow buyers to make a deal that would not otherwise be possible. A seller may also be attracted by the interest that can be earned with a loan secured by the old home.

But seller financing is not always workable. Many sellers need money from their sale to buy a new home or for other purposes. Even when seller financing is available, the monthly payments are an expense that lenders will count when they compute front and back ratios.

BROKER TAKE-BACKS

The broker is another party interested in the sale and, like a seller, to make a deal work he or she will sometimes loan money to a purchaser. Because the broker typically works for the seller, however, loans to a purchaser are only possible when the seller approves such financing in advance.

If a broker lists and sells a home for $150,000 and receives a 6 percent commission, that's $9,000 which might be available to the buyer. And while $9,000 might not be much in the context of a $150,000 sale, it's a sizable amount when $30,000 is needed for a 20 percent down payment.

As a practical matter, broker loans are rarely available. While 6 percent of $150,000 is $9,000, in many cases the money is split between a broker and an agent, or split between two brokers and two agents. Still, if you need cash to close a deal, there's no harm asking if the broker can provide a loan.

NO MONEY DOWN

No book on real estate would be complete these days without mentioning deals with no money down. While VA loans are clearly one way to buy without money up front, those who advocate deals with no money down rarely discuss VA financing alone. Instead, they propose financing strategies that are not only outside the mainstream of real estate finance, they are also outside the realm of plausibility.

A deal with no money down might work like this: The Ford home is being sold for $100,000. The buyer offers $75,000, but only if he can take over the seller's current $50,000 FHA mortgage and if the seller will take back a $25,000 loan. When the deal is presented in writing, the seller is likely to discover that the buyer also wants the seller to pay all closing costs and loan expenses.

Another strategy works this way: The seller is offered something other than a cash down payment, perhaps gemstones of uncommon quality—that is, not as much quality as the stones sold by jewelers.

No-money-down schemes sound good on TV and in seminars, but first-time buyers need to be aware that promoters are interested in selling tape recordings and seminar seats, not real estate. If no-money-down plans worked so well, if everyone who attended a seminar succeeded in real estate, then everyone would buy property without cash or credit, lenders would be unnecessary, first-time buyers could readily finance houses, and the country would be overrun with millionaires.

What often happens is that no-money-downers go to those areas where real estate values are falling. Owners in such communities are delighted to sell with no money down, if only to unload their property. Once purchased, buyers have a choice of living in the property (and then trying to find a job in a declining region) or renting it (in an environment where rents are cheap because many owners are competing for tenants).

If the local economy turns around, it is then possible to sell the property at a profit. Of course, if the local area does not grow, if people and businesses continue to move out, if rents stay level or fall relative to the cost of living, then it will be the buyer's turn to sell to someone else, perhaps with no money down.

Try to buy property without cash in an area where the economy is expanding and the results are likely to be far different. Because the area is growing, there's a demand for housing, and sellers will have many ready, willing, and able buyers—people qualified to borrow and willing to pay market values.

It's fair to say that deals with no money down do happen from time to time in markets where real estate values are rising, but it is reasonable to point out that such sales, like lottery winners, are rare. As for those few deals that do take place, one has to wonder how many involve ignorant or terribly desperate sellers.

It's something to sleep on. If you can.

CO-SIGNERS

To this point we have looked at financing alternatives that depend on buyer resources, an often unworkable dependency in high-priced areas. We can change the game rules, however, by using the income and assets of other players.

When the Maxwells needed financing to buy a home in southern California they quickly confirmed what everyone already knew: Homes that typically started at $300,000 or more are simply unaffordable even for a couple earning $80,000 a year.

No one is suggesting that $80,000 is evidence of poverty or that most households would not be pleased with such earnings, but the reality is that areas where high incomes are possible are also areas where housing costs are steep.

The Maxwells face a difficult choice. They can buy farther away from their work, but farther away translates into four hours a day on the highway, 20 hours a week of otherwise productive time, to say nothing of vast irritation and annoyance.

Rather than commute insane distances, the Maxwells do what many young families do: They call Mom and Dad. It isn't a down payment they need; frugal living has been rewarded with $90,000 in savings. They want their parents to co-sign a mortgage; in effect, they want to use their parents' credit and income to qualify for a loan.

Co-signing a mortgage is not a casual event. If the loan is defaulted, the co-signers are fully liable for the debt. But the young Maxwells have shown they can both earn and save, property values are rising, and so Mom and Dad gladly agree to co-sign.

To act as co-signers, the elder Maxwells apply for a loan with their children and, with the incomes from two households, the lender's requirements are easily met.

Before speaking to parents or others about co-signing, first-time buyers should ask about lender policies. Co-signing is attractive to lenders because there are more warm bodies to go after if the property must be foreclosed and therefore less risk. Conversely, some lenders are wary of co-signers and allow only parents or other relatives to co-sign.

Even with a parental co-signer, first-time buyers may be required to put up 5 or 10 percent of the total purchase price with their *own* money. If a parental co-signer is also a gift donor, then first-time buyers must ask whether the gift is counted as part of the buyer's funds or whether the purchaser must come up with additional cash.

Lenders often insist that loan co-signers also appear as co-owners, but the problem with co-ownership is that multiple owners must decide how bills will be paid, how profits will be divided, how tax benefits will be shared, and what happens if someone dies. These are significant issues which require legal advice, a written agreement between co-signers, and a will for each co-owner.

If you purchase with a co-signer, be certain to apply for financing and hold title as individuals. Most residential lenders are prepared to deal with "natural" people, but throw in a partnership or corporation ("unnatural" people) and many lenders will regard the transaction as a commercial venture subject to commercial rates and underwriting standards.

EQUITY-SHARING

Although many first-time buyers lack capital and income, they do have an asset that can lead to property ownership: occupancy.

It might seem as though occupancy is an altogether common value, something available from any renter. But renters and owners have an adversarial relationship. One wants more rent, the other wants to pay less. For property owners there are management, repair, and collection costs, expenses that can be reduced with good tenants, and no tenant is better than one with an ownership interest.

With an occupant co-owner a manager is unnecessary, repairs can be made by the occupant, and collecting monthly payments should be easy. In addition, investor access to low-cost residential financing can be available when one owner lives on the property.

When investors and first-time buyers purchase real estate together each obtains access to assets that might otherwise be unavailable. Investors are people with cash and income, the very resources first-time buyers often lack. First-time buyers are ideal residents who represent less risk and hassle than tenants without equity interests. We can combine the strengths of both investors and first-time purchasers in a process called *equity-sharing*.

To see how equity-sharing works, consider a situation where an investor and a first-time buyer purchase a small single-family home for $100,000. Each party puts up $5,000 plus closing costs and the balance is financed with a residential mortgage. Each party has a 50 percent property interest in our example, though uneven interests are possible.

In an equity-sharing arrangement, the first-time buyer must use the property as a *principal residence.* In exchange for the property's use, the first-time buyer—now a resident co-owner—makes two forms of monthly payments.

First, there is a payment to the lender equal to 50 percent of the monthly mortgage, taxes, and insurance, say $475.

Second, there is a payment to the investor co-owner, perhaps $525 in this case. The investor must receive a *fair market* rent for his or her share of the property because he has a 50 percent property interest, property used entirely by the resident co-owner. If he does not receive a fair market rent, then the deal is not an equity-sharing arrangement and certain tax benefits will be unavailable.

The investor receives $525, but he also has to pay for his share of the mortgage, taxes, insurance, and other costs. (See Table 19.)

At the end of each year the resident co-owner can deduct his costs for mortgage interest and property taxes when computing his taxes. The investor can deduct his expenses for mortgage interest, property taxes, insurance, repairs, and depreciation for half the property. When the property is sold, the co-owners will

Table 19   EQUITY SHARING

Purchase Price	$100,000
Down Payment	$10,000
Loan Amount	$90,000
Interest Rate	10.5 percent
Monthly Loan Payment	$823.27
Fair Market Rent	$1,050.00
Investor Share	50 percent
Investor Income	$525

split any profit according to their share in the property. The resident co-owner can then defer taxes by purchasing a personal residence of equal or greater value, while the investor must report his profits and pay all required taxes.

First-time buyers will need a written contract to create an equity-sharing agreement, a contract that should be written or reviewed by a knowledgeable attorney.

First-time buyers should be aware that to be successful, equity-sharing must make sense on several different levels.

As a business deal, equity-sharing must produce an investor benefit such as tax write-offs, monthly income, the potential for appreciation, or all three.

As a home, the property must be attractive, a place where you want to live and which meets your needs.

A property purchased with an equity-sharing agreement will be attractive to some lenders, but not others. Speak with loan officers to see how your deal matches lender requirements. Major issues include your cash contribution and an agreement not to sell the property for a given time period, say five or seven years. Note that while lenders often want co-buyers to establish a minimum ownership period in an equity-sharing agreement, the period desired by lenders and the intended ownership term required for tax purposes may differ. Speak to an attorney or CPA for details.

Equity-sharing will be most attractive to investors if both occupancy and labor are included in the deal. If you are willing to paint, fix up, and repair, then it becomes possible to find a home in poor physical condition, improve it, and pocket the new and higher value that a home in pristine condition can command. Local brokers may be able to find equity-sharing partners, locate suitable properties, and suggest lenders who make such deals in your area. In addition to brokers, equity-sharing investors can sometimes be found at home. Instead of an outright gift, perhaps your parents would prefer an equity-sharing arrangement that offers both tax benefits and the potential for profit.

MINGLES

Not only can first-time buyers purchase real estate with co-signers and with co-owners, it's also possible to go a step further and purchase as both co-owners and co-occupants.

Buying together and living together is more than a real estate deal, but assuming that personal relations are not contentious, then buying a mingles property can be attractive.

With a mingles property there are two or more owners. Each owner lives at the property and each has separate space.

Many properties designed as single-family homes are suitable for mingles units. The best choice is a house with a separate wing or unit so that each purchaser has total independence and privacy.

Townhouses can be used as mingles units, especially when there are basement living quarters. One buyer lives on the second floor where there may be two or three bedrooms while another owner lives in the basement. Both owners share the kitchen, dining room, and living room. The best townhouses for this purpose will have sunny, walk-out basements with full baths.

Apartment-style condominiums are sometimes designed as mingles units with two master bedroom suites separated by a common living room, dining room, and kitchen. By definition, apartment-style condos are likely to have less privacy and less space than a three-story townhouse.

Multi-unit properties can also be used as mingles. Two people can buy a duplex, a property with two separate units under a single roof. Duplex units are typically equal in size, identical in design, and blessed with separate entrances.

First-time buyers may also want to consider a triplex, a property with three units. Each owner lives in one unit, and the remaining space can be rented out to cut ownership costs. The same system can be used with a fourplex, a property with four units.

Once buyers begin to look at more than four units the picture changes. Buy one to four units, live on the property, and attractive financing is often available. Buy five units or more and you have a commercial deal with different rates, terms, and rules.

A properly designed mingles unit coupled with compatible owners can be attractive to first-time buyers. Rather than buying a complete property, purchasers can acquire an affordable real estate interest at a time when steep costs or high interest rates might otherwise make ownership impossible.

6

ARMs as Income Alternatives

We have seen that the requirement to pay 20 percent down can be side-stepped with insurance plans, guarantee programs, and gifts. It follows that if cash demands can be minimized, something can also be done to reduce income requirements.

The need for income can be seen from two perspectives. Up front, income is important because the more you have, the more you can borrow. Over time, you need income to make monthly payments.

In considering the income issue, lenders look for steady earnings now and the probability of steady income in the future. Regular income growth is certainly a plus, as is income derived from substantially the same activity over several years. As to a single win at the racetrack or an inheritance, while such money might help with a down payment, it can hardly be regarded as income.

When we looked at conventional financing we saw that lenders have very definite ideas about down payments and qualifying ratios. We also saw why. Conventional, fixed-rate loans present major risks to lenders.

One risk is reduced buying power. As we saw in Chapter 5, with fixed-rate financing lenders are paid the same number of dollars each month, even though the purchasing power of money can decline.

Not only do conventional loans represent eroding buying power for lenders, they can also destabilize lender finances.

Long-term mortgages are financed with short-term debt. The lender who makes 30-year, fixed-rate loans underwrites such mortgages with short-term borrowing. When you open a passbook savings account or take out a certificate of deposit, you're really making a short-term loan to a lender. The lender takes your money and money from other people, combines the funds, and then underwrites long-term loans.

If 30-year financing is now available with a 10 percent interest rate, then lenders must pay less for savings accounts and certificates to make a profit. If the combination of business expenses and short-term interest rates exceeds 10 percent, then the lender loses money in this example. (See Table 20.)

The problem is that lenders don't always get sufficient returns on their money. In the late 1970s and early 1980s, lenders who held hundreds of billions of dollars in long-term loans watched as interest rates rose to historic heights. In both 1980 and 1981, the prime rate topped 20 percent. Meanwhile, lender portfolios included loans where borrowers were paying 6, 7, 8, and 9 percent interest. In other words, while borrowers were obligated to pay low interest rates set many years before, lenders were forced to underwrite long-term loans at *current* rates. Borrowing money at 4 percent to earn 6, 7, or 8 percent is good business. Borrowing money at 20 percent to earn 6, 7, or 8 percent is a disaster.

Because of declining buying power and the potential for soaring short-term interest rates, lenders have distanced themselves from 30-year, fixed-rate loans. Some no longer offer conventional financing, while others discourage borrowers with high rates and tough qualification standards.

Instead of guessing about future interest levels, lenders have increasingly turned to *adjustable rate mortgages,* or ARMs, loans

Table 20   UNDERWRITING FIXED-RATE LOANS

1. Lender collects passbook savings accounts, NOW accounts, demand deposits, etc.

2. Lender pays 7.5 percent interest on short-term funds.

3. Lender creates long-term mortgages at 10 percent.

4. Lender uses 2.5 percent margin for business expenses.

5. Some portion of the 2.5 percent margin, one hopes, is the lender's profit.

where the interest rate varies. With interest rates that can move, it's the borrower rather than the lender who must now worry about changing interest levels.

It's clear that fixed-rate loans are a better deal for borrowers than ARMs, assuming interest rates and qualification standards are equal. The catch is that interest rates and qualification standards are not identical and therefore ARMs allow purchasers to make larger loans than fixed-rate financing.

- Rather than a fixed interest rate, ARM interest levels can move up and down throughout the entire loan term.

- Rather than steady payments, monthly costs can rise and fall.

- Rather than a 15- or 30-year term, some ARMs can stretch to as long as 40 years.

- Rather than self-amortization, some ARMs can evolve into *balloon loans.* With balloon financing, when the loan term ends money is still owed to the lender.

- Rather than self-amortization, some ARMs allow negative amortization. *Negative amortization* means that if monthly payments do not cover costs, the amount not covered is added to the outstanding principal. For example, a $125,000 mortgage will require monthly payments of $1,096.96 at 10 percent interest over 30 years. If a borrower makes a $1,000 payment, then the $96.96 difference will be added to the debt. The next month, interest will be figured on the basis of a debt worth $125,096.96.

- ARMs, unlike fixed-rate loans, are generally assumable at current rates and terms as long as the lender approves the new borrower.

- ARM lenders typically encourage prepayments without penalty. Unlike fixed-rate loans where monthly payments never change, prepaying an ARM can result in lower monthly costs.

The most basic distinction between ARMs and fixed-rate financing is how rates are established. With fixed-rate loans there is one interest rate and that rate is established up front.

With ARMs the rate is set differently. (See Table 21.)

Table 21   CREATING AN ADJUSTABLE RATE MORTGAGE

Index + Margin = Rate
7.5 Percent Index + 2.5 Percent Margin = 10 Percent Rate

First, an index is selected. Common indexes include the 11th District Cost of Funds, one-year treasury securities, and 30-year rates for fixed-rate and adjustable loans calculated by the Federal Home Loan Mortgage Corporation (FHLMC). These rates are published regularly in many newspapers, including the "Money" section in *USA Today*.

Second, a margin is selected and added to the index. During the ARM's life, while the index may move up or down, the margin never changes. If the margin is 2.5 percent and the index one year is 7.5 percent, then the interest rate is 10 percent (7.5 plus 2.5). If the index rises to 8 percent, then the interest rate goes up to 10.5 percent (8 plus 2.5).

The idea that rates can change raises two important questions. First, how often are rates changed? Second, how high can they go?

Rates may change as often as every month under some programs. Other ARMs have adjustment periods every 6, 12, or 36 months.

Interest rate changes are typically controlled by two types of caps. There is a rate cap for each adjustment period, perhaps 1 percent every 6 months or 2 percent every 12 months. There is also a lifetime cap, typically 4 to 6 percent above the start rate.

Thus when a lender says you can have "a 1-year ARM with 2/4 caps and an 8 percent start rate," you can get ARM financing that has an initial interest rate of 8 percent for one year. The rate changes each year and can go up or down no more than 2 percent a year. The top rate for this loan is 12 percent (the 8 percent start rate plus the 4 percent lifetime cap).

Not only are there *interest* caps, but many ARMS also have *payment* caps. A typical payment cap might be 7.5 percent for each adjustment period.

Suppose a $100,000 loan has an 8 percent start rate, a 2 percent adjustment cap, and a 7.5 percent payment cap. Suppose also that in the second year, the interest rate moves up 2 percentage points to 10 percent. How much does the borrower owe each month?

In our example, at 8 percent interest over 30 years, the borrower is paying $733.76 per month. If the interest rate rises to 10 percent, the borrower should pay $877.57 a month. But since there's a 7.5 percent payment cap, the most monthly payments can rise is 7.5 percent, or $55.03 in this case ($733.76 × 7.5 percent). If we take the base payment ($733.76) and add the maximum allowable amount ($55.03), then the most the borrower can be required to pay is $788.79.

The difference between $788.79 and $877.57 is $88.78, money that would go to the lender were it not for the payment cap. Some ARM lenders, however, regard the $88.78 as negative amortization.

If negative amortization is allowed, the loan works this way: In the second year the borrower pays either $788.79 per month or $877.57 a month. If the borrower elects to pay the smaller amount, then $88.78 is added to the principal balance.

Given this maze of rates, caps, and adjustments, why would any borrower pick an ARM over fixed-rate financing? For many borrowers, especially those buying a home for the first time, ARMs may be the only financing available.

With a fixed-rate loan lenders typically qualify borrowers with 28/36 ratios. With ARMs, many lenders use more liberal ratios, perhaps 33/38 or even 36/42 with 90 percent financing.

Not only are ARM ratios more liberal, they're likely to be based on lower up-front start rates. If fixed-rate mortgages are available at 10.5 percent, then ARMs may start with an 8 percent interest rate. Some lenders will qualify applicants with the start rate (8 percent), while others may add 1 percent. In this example, if 1 percent is added to the start rate, then the qualifying rate will be 9 percent.

To see how low start rates influence affordability, consider a $100,000 mortgage. If the ratios are 28/36 and the rate for fixed-rate financing is 10.5 percent, then the monthly cost for principal and interest will be $914.74. If we add $30 a month for insurance and $125 a month for taxes, then the PITI for this loan is $1,069.74 and an income of at least $45,846 will be required to qualify.

If we have an ARM where the qualifying rate is 9 percent and the ratios are 33/38, then the situation changes. Now the qualifying cost for principal and interest is just $804.62. Add insurance ($30) and taxes ($125), and the total *qualifying* expense for PITI is $959.62. Using more liberal ratios, someone with an income of $34,895 can afford this loan. (See Table 22.)

If we worked this same example and said, as some lenders do, that the start rate and the qualifying rate are the same, the income requirement will drop even further. With an 8 percent qualifying ratio, the monthly cost for principal and interest totals $733.76. Add $155 per month for taxes and insurance, and PITI is $888.76. Using 33/38 ratios, a borrower will need an income of at least $32,319 to qualify for this loan.

The examples above show that with ARMs an individual earning $32,500 can qualify for as much financing as a fixed-rate borrower who earns $45,850. Since the population of people who make $33,000 a year is much greater than the number who make $46,000, ARM popularity is easy to understand, especially when interest rates are high.

ARMs, INTEREST CAPS, AND THE WORST CASE

Lenders today aggressively market ARMs, a marketing preference that can be advantageous to first-time buyers in many ways. The fact is that *selected* ARMs are often the best loan options for purchasers, especially those who do not intend to own their first property for more than a few years.

To understand why, consider a period where the interest

Table 22   LIBERAL LOANS MEAN MORE BORROWING POWER

Loan Amount	$100,000	$100,000
Loan Term	30 years, fixed rate	30 years, ARM
Interest Rate	10.5 percent	9 percent
Monthly Payment	$914.74	$804.62
Taxes	$125.00	$125.00
Insurance	$30.00	$30.00
PITI	$1,069.74	$959.62
Front Ratio	28 percent	33 percent
Minimum Income	$45,846	$34,895

level for fixed-rate financing is 10.5 percent while 1-year ARMs start at 8 percent. Let's assume that $100,000 is borrowed for 30 years and that the ARM has interest caps of 2 percent per adjustment period and 4 percent over the loan's life. There is no *payment* cap and negative amortization is not allowed. Here's what happens in the *worst* case. (See Table 23.)

- In year 1, the monthly cost for principal and interest with the ARM is $733.76. The monthly cost for the fixed-rate loan is $914.74.

- In year 2, the ARM interest rate rises to 10 percent. The monthly cost for principal and interest is $875.11. The monthly cost for the fixed-rate loan is $914.74.

- In year 3, the ARM interest cost rises to 12 percent and the monthly cost for principal and interest is $1,021.61. The monthly cost for the fixed-rate loan is $914.74.

- In year 4, the ARM interest cost is still 12 percent and principal and interest cost $1,021.61. The monthly cost for the fixed-rate

Table 23 ARMS WITH INTEREST CAPS VERSUS CONVENTIONAL FINANCING: WORST-CASE EXAMPLE

	ARM	Conventional Loan
Loan Amount	$100,000	$100,000
First Year Interest Rate Payment	8 percent $733.76	10.5 percent $914.74
Second Year Interest Rate Payment	10 percent $875.11	10.5 percent $914.74
Third Year Interest Rate Payment	12 percent $1,021.61	10.5 percent $914.74
Fourth Year Interest Rate Payment	12 percent $1,021.61	10.5 percent $914.74
Fifth Year Interest Rate Payment	12 percent $1,021.61	10.5 percent $914.74

loan remains $914.74. Note that the ARM cannot rise above 12 percent because there is a 4 percent lifetime cap (an 8 percent start rate plus 4 percent equals 12 percent).

■ In year 5, the ARM continues at 12 percent and the monthly cost is $1,021.61. The monthly cost for the fixed-rate loan is still $914.74.

As we look at these two loans it's clear that in the worst possible case, after two years the ARM borrower will face higher monthly costs. But we might also look at these loans from a different perspective.

Suppose a borrower sells the property in five or fewer years. How do the loans compare if we look at *total costs* for principal and interest? (See Table 24.)

Table 24   CASH COSTS: ARM VERSUS CONVENTIONAL FINANCING: WORST-CASE EXAMPLE

	ARM	*Conventional Loan*
Loan Amount	$100,000	$100,000
First Year		
Interest Rate	8 percent	10.5 percent
Cash Cost	$8,805.12	$10,976.87
Savings to Date	$2,171.75	0
Second Year		
Interest Rate	10 percent	10.5 percent
Cash Cost	$10,501.32	$10,976.87
Savings to Date	$2,647.30	0
Third Year		
Interest Rate	12 percent	10.5 percent
Cash Cost	$12,259.32	$10,976.87
Savings To Date	$1,364.85	0
Fourth Year		
Interest Rate	12 percent	10.5 percent
Cash Cost	$12,259.32	$10,976.87
Savings to Date	$82.40	0
Fifth Year		
Interest Rate	12 percent	10.5 percent
Cash Cost	$12,259.32	$10,976.87
Savings to Date	0	$1,200.05

- In year 1, the ARM has a total cost of $8,805.12. The fixed-rate borrower has paid out $10,976.87. After one year the ARM borrower is ahead by $2,171.75

- In year 2, ARM payments total $10,501.32. The fixed-rate loan still costs $10,976.87 per year, so after two years the ARM borrower is ahead by $2,647.30.

- In year 3, ARM payments plateau at $12,259.32. Compared to fixed-rate costs ($10,976.87), the ARM borrower loses ground and is now ahead by just $1,364.85.

- In year 4, the ARM and fixed-rate costs are the same as year 3. Now the ARM borrower is ahead by just $82.40.

- In year 5, we again repeat the costs found in year 3, $12,259.32 for the ARM and $10,976.87 for the fixed-rate loan. After five years the fixed-rate borrower is ahead by $1,200.05.

This example shows that even though the particular ARM we described has the *potential* to cost more than fixed-rate financing, after four years the ARM borrower pays out less cash, *even in the worst possible case.*

This example can also explain several other factors which make ARMs extremely interesting to first-time borrowers.

First, it's entirely possible that the ARM will never reach its upper interest cap and that the cash benefit projected above will be even larger.

Second, it's also possible that over time the average ARM interest rate will be less than 10.5 percent. Should this happen, the ARM will always be a better deal than the fixed-rate loan.

Third, even in the worst case, ARM savings are bunched up front, precisely where they have the most value for first-time homebuyers who are often cash-short.

ARMS AND PAYMENT CAPS

So far we have seen what happens in the worst case when a fixed-rate loan and an ARM with an interest cap are compared. Even more interesting are the results which develop when fixed-rate financing is compared with an ARM that employs a *payment* cap.

Suppose that we have two loans available, each for $100,000 and each for a 30-year term. Suppose a fixed-rate mortgage is priced at 10.5 percent interest while a 1-year ARM has the following terms: a 2 percent annual and a 4 percent lifetime interest cap, no negative amortization, and an 8 percent start rate. In addition, the ARM has a 7.5 percent annual payment cap.

With this loan, the annual payment cap takes precedence over the interest caps, a situation which creates a very attractive loan package. This is how an ARM and a fixed-rate loan match up over five years, assuming that interest rates rise as much as possible each year. (See Table 25.)

- In year 1, the ARM has monthly costs of $733.76, while the fixed-rate loan costs $914.74. The ARM borrower saves $2,171.76.

Table 25 ARM WITH 7.5 PERCENT PAYMENT CAP VERSUS
CONVENTIONAL FINANCING: WORST-CASE EXAMPLE

	ARM	*Conventional Loan*
Loan Amount	$100,000	$100,000
First Year		
Interest Rate	8 percent	10.5 percent
Payment	$733.76	$914.74
Savings to Date	$2,171.76	0
Second Year		
Interest Rate	10 percent	10.5 percent
Payment	$788.79	$914.74
Savings to Date	$3,863.16	0
Third Year		
Interest Rate	12 percent	10.5 percent
Payment	$847.95	$914.74
Savings to Date	$4,484.64	0
Fourth Year		
Interest Rate	12 percent	10.5 percent
Payment	$911.55	$914.74
Savings to Date	$4,522.92	0
Fifth Year		
Interest Rate	12 percent	10.5 percent
Payment	$979.91	$914.74
Savings to Date	$3,742.08	0

- In year 2, the ARM rate rises to 10 percent. If the borrower paid at the 10 percent rate, the monthly cost for this loan should be $875.11. With a 7.5 percent payment cap the monthly cost for principal and interest can only rise to $788.79. ($733.76 plus $55.03; the $55.03 is 7.5 percent of $733.76). The fixed-rate loan still has monthly costs of $914.74. The ARM borrower saves $1,511.40, a total of $3,683.16 over two years.

  In the second year we can see the maximum monthly payments will not even cover interest costs, much less reduce the loan balance. We now have a situation where only interest is being paid and the outstanding debt remains unchanged.

- In year 3, the ARM interest rate rises to 12 percent, the maximum allowed under the lifetime interest cap. The monthly payment increases to $847.95 while the fixed-rate loan still costs $914.74 per month. In year 3, the ARM is $801.48 less expensive than the fixed-rate loan. Over three years the ARM borrower is ahead by $4,484.64. As in the second year, the loan balance remains unchanged.

- In year 4, ARM payments rise to $911.55. The fixed-rate loan again has monthly costs of $914.74, so the ARM borrower saves $38.28 during the year. At the end of four years the ARM borrower is still ahead by $4,522.92.

- In year 5, ARM payments rise to $979.81, an amount that at last exceeds the fixed-rate loan. For the year, the fixed-rate loan saves $780.84 when compared with the ARM. Over the five-year term, however, the ARM still saves $3,742.08.

It took five years for the fixed-rate loan to beat the ARM in a *worst-case* scenario, but one has to ask: How realistic is a worst-case situation? Surely the worst case represents the extreme, the events least likely to occur.

While the fixed-rate loan in this example is potentially less expensive than the ARM over a 30-year period, it is absolutely more expensive in the first years of ownership, the time when buyers are most likely to need as much cash as possible. In latter years, presumably, buyer income will rise and increased ARM costs can be absorbed more easily.

But whether a fixed-rate loan is a better deal over a period of three decades is largely irrelevant. The fact is that the overwhelming majority of buyers do not own homes for 30 years. Since many first-time buyers only expect to own their first home for five years or less, *selected* ARMs offer inherent advantages short-term borrowers should not overlook.

ARMS AND RE-CASTING

In the example with the 7.5 percent payment cap we saw that while monthly costs were contained, the loan quickly evolved into an interest-only mortgage where the principal balance did not decline. After five years, the ARM debt totaled $99,164.69 while the principal outstanding with the fixed-rate loan was $96,881.65—a difference of $2,283.04, or much of the money that was "saved" in monthly ARM payments.

As monthly payments rise 7.5 percent a year they will ultimately reach a point where the outstanding debt begins to decline. The problem is that if a loan has a payment cap, a high lifetime cap, *and* interest rates remain at steep levels, it is possible that loan reductions might not occur for many years.

Rather than have a loan with a large outstanding balance, and rather than lose interest because of payment caps, ARMs often contain a *re-casting* provision.

In our worst-case example with the 7.5 percent payment cap, we saw that after five years monthly payments had risen to $979.91 while the outstanding debt stood at $99,164.69, a principal reduction of merely $835.31! If interest in the sixth year continues at 12 percent, and if monthly payments rise another 7.5 percent, the borrower will pay $1,053.40 per month.

But with a re-casting provision, the lender recalculates the loan based on the current interest rate (12 percent in our worst-case example) and the outstanding loan amount ($99,164.69). To pay the loan over 25 years—the time remaining under the mortgage term—the monthly payments must total $1,044.43.

Because the loan amount in this example is as high as it can go, and because the interest rate is also at the highest level possible under the lifetime cap, the monthly cost will not exceed $1,044.43. Each payment in the coming year, at least, will reduce the mortgage balance. If it also happens that interest rates fall, if they are not at the highest levels, the monthly cost will decline significantly.

It may seem that re-casting produces substantially higher monthly costs than borrowers might expect with fixed-rate loans. But if the thought of higher rates five years from now seems discomforting, consider these ideas:

- Five years from now borrowers, especially first-time homebuyers, should have larger incomes.

- Over a five-year period inflation will reduce money's buying power, thus offsetting higher cash costs.

- If property values rise, then the ability to secure an appreciating asset at low cost should not be overlooked. If property values decline, both lenders and borrowers will be unhappy—borrowers because they have less equity, lenders because they have less security.

- Compared to a fixed-rate cost of $914.74 a month in our example, a $1,044.43 monthly bill for principal and interest six years later means that mortgage costs have increased by an average of only 2.23 percent annually in a worst-case situation. Most renters would probably be elated if rental costs rose less than 3 percent a year and many first-time buyers would be renters if it were not for the availability of adjustable-rate mortgages.

- Our example forecasts that with the worst possible conditions mortgage costs will decline after the sixth year. Few people would suggest lower rental rates six years from now.

ARMS AND NEGATIVE AMORTIZATION

While payment and interest caps can be used to control monthly costs, first-time buyers need to watch principal balances as well. *Some ARMs hold down monthly payments while allowing debt to increase,* a process known as *negative amortization.*

In our examples we saw that monthly payments generally represent both principal and interest, except when interest rates are high. With high rates and caps, it's possible to have a situation where monthly payments represent interest only, as the example with 7.5 percent payment caps showed.

But suppose the loan terms are changed. Suppose we have an

ARM that works like this: Each monthly payment will be used for principal and interest. However, if interest rates rise faster than payments, any interest unpaid during a given month will be added to the loan balance as negative amortization.

How does a loan with negative amortization work? Let's compare a fixed-rate 10.5 percent interest loan with a "neg am" ARM. The ARM has an 8 percent start rate, a 7.5-percent payment cap, a 2 percent annual cap, and a 12 percent lifetime cap. Both are $100,000 mortgages and both have 30-year terms. (See Table 26.)

Table 26 NEGATIVE AMORTIZATION AT WORK: WORST-CASE EXAMPLE

	ARM	*Conventional Loan*
Loan Amount	$100,000	$100,000
First Year		
Interest Rate	8 percent	10.5 percent
Payment	$733.76	$914.74
Savings to Date	$2,171.76	0
Loan Balance	$99,164.69	$99,499.49
Second Year		
Interest Rate	10 percent	10.5 percent
Payment	$788.79	$914.74
Savings to Date	$3,863.16	0
Loan Balance	$99,633.54	$98,943.82
Third Year		
Interest Rate	12 percent	10.5 percent
Payment	$847.95	$914.74
Savings to Date	$4,484.64	0
Loan Balance	$101,515.42	$98,326.91
Fourth Year		
Interest Rate	12 percent	10.5 percent
Payment	$911.55	$914.74
Savings to Date	$4,522.92	0
Loan Balance	$102,829.40	$97,642.02
Fifth Year		
Interest Rate	12 percent	10.5 percent
Payment	$979.91	$914.74
Savings to Date	$3,742.08	0
Loan Balance	$103,442.99	$96,881.65

- In year 1, the ARM has monthly costs of $733.76 while the fixed-rate loan costs $914.74. The ARM borrower saves $2,171.76. Loan balances decline with both loans; in fact, an ARM borrower actually cuts the loan balance more than the individual who uses fixed-rate financing ($99,164.69 versus $99,499.49).

- In year 2, the ARM rate rises to 10 percent but the monthly cost only goes up to $788.79 because of the payment cap. Since this figure is lower than the full interest cost, negative amortization begins and the loan balance rises each month. At the end of the second year, the ARM loan balance is up to $99,633.54 while the fixed-rate loan is down to $98,943.82. Because of lower monthly payments, however, the ARM borrower saves $1,511.40 in cash and is ahead by $3,683.16 in monthly payments over two years.

- In year 3, the ARM interest rate reaches the 12 percent maximum, but the monthly payment is only $847.95. Negative amortization for the year reaches $1,881.88 and the loan balance increases to $101,515.42—more than the amount originally borrowed! On the basis of monthly costs, however, the ARM borrower is ahead by $4,484.64 after three years.

- In year 4, ARM payments are set at $911.55, still not enough to reduce the debt. In the fourth year negative amortization continues and the loan balance reaches $102,829.40. The fixed-rate loan balance at this point has dropped to $97,642.02—a $5,187.38 difference when compared with the neg am ARM. At the end of four years the ARM borrower still has a payment advantage of $4,522.92.

- In year 5 the monthly expense for the ARM rises to $979.91, more than the fixed-rate borrower pays, but even so, negative amortization continues. After the fifth year, the ARM balance is $103,442.99 while the fixed-rate borrower owes just $96,881.65.

Over the five-year period two trends emerge.

First, on the basis of monthly costs the ARM still costs $3,742.08 less than the fixed-rate loan.

Second, the fixed-rate loan balance is $6,561.34 less than the ARM.

Can a negative amortization loan be a good deal?

To accept the greater risks and potential costs represented by neg am loans, first-time buyers should be able to require the best possible rates and terms. Even then, negative amortization loans only make sense in markets where property values are rising now and can reasonably be expected to rise for many years.

Also, it should be said that even though an ARM may permit negative amortization, *unlike our example such amortization may not occur if interest rates do not constantly reach worst-case levels.*

ARMs that permit negative amortization commonly allow borrowers to make three types of monthly payments. First, borrowers can make regular payments, say $1,000. Second, interest-only payments can be made in those cases where the interest level exceeds the regular payment. For example, if the required payment is $1,000 but the monthly interest cost is $1,050, a borrower can make a $1,000 payment. Third, borrowers can prepay loans. If $1,000 is required each month and a borrower pays $1,100, then the loan balance can decline. Borrowers faced with negative amortization can thus adjust their payments according to how much they want to spend each month and whether they feel principal reductions are important.

Loans that feature negative amortization typically contain a five-year re-casting provision so monthly payments can be reset. For a mortgage with a $103,442.99 balance, a 12 percent interest rate, and 25 years to go, the monthly payment will be $1,089.49—$174.75 per month more than a $100,000, 30-year fixed-rate loan at 10.5 percent interest, or an additional cost of almost $2,100 a year.

INDEXES AND ARM COSTS

While rate and payment caps limit risks associated with ARMs, there's another factor that can also moderate ARM payments: the basic index used to compute interest rates.

An index is an independent measure beyond lender control, thereby assuring that rates do not rise unfairly or artificially. Over the years several indexes have been used, some of which favor borrowers less than others.

One idea has been to tie ARM rates to the prime rate, the

interest level traditionally defined as the rate lenders provide for their "best" customers. This rate, however, is set by the lender in response to the lender's perception of market conditions, a perception likely to be influenced by inherent self-interest.

A somewhat similar approach, using another lender's prime rate, merely disguises the problem, since other lenders may also benefit from higher rates.

A more distant measure is the weighted average value for given treasury issues. Since these rates are determined at public auction, and since the Treasury Department has an extreme interest in holding down interest rates, treasury securities are attractive. Such securities, however, compete with alternative investments and therefore may rise or fall with great speed.

Some lenders compute rates according to figures published by the Federal Home Loan Bank Board, a governmental instrument that oversees federally chartered savings and loan associations. Such figures reflect current interest levels and are often used to calculate fixed rates for convertible ARMs.

Another choice is the rate established by the Federal Home Loan Bank in San Francisco, one of 12 district banks that are part of the Office of Thrift Supervision. Known as the 11th District Cost of Funds Index, or the 11th District COF, this index reflects the interest rates paid by approximately 200 savings and loan associations in California, Arizona, and Nevada for the use of depositor funds and other monies.

Borrowers throughout the country have increasingly turned to the 11th District COF because it tends to move up—and down—with less speed than other indexes. It also tends to avoid the peaks and valleys that other indexes reach. For example, in 1981 when the prime rate reached 20.5 percent, the index for 6-month treasury bills stood at 17.06 percent and the 11th District rate was just 12.029 percent.

ARMS AND CAUTION

There's little doubt that ARMs can be attractive to first-time buyers, especially when they employ liberal ratios and rely on low start rates.

But ARMs can lose such charm when not aggressively priced. If fixed-rate loans are set at 10.5 percent and 1-year ARMs begin at 9.5 percent, who needs them? A 1 percent gap between fixed-rate financing and ARMs is not large enough to justify the risks ARMs represent.

For those borrowers who have a choice, who can qualify for both fixed-rate and adjustable financing, ARMs should be avoided unless they offer observable benefits over a five-year period, assuming that interest rates always go to the highest allowable levels. Observable benefits include lower total costs, lower monthly payments for at least three or four years, and faster amortization.

If observable benefits are not there, forget ARMs.

MARGINS, POINTS, AND PRICING

The description "a good loan" is often defined by interest levels and points. We have already seen (Chapter 4) that points and interest can be traded back and forth to produce attractive loans. But can we go a step further? Can we trade points for a lower margin?

Trading points for lower margins is rare, though some lenders have offered such deals from time to time. For first-time buyers, the availability of such trades may be extremely attractive, especially if the *seller* will pay some or all of the points.

Suppose we have a loan with a 2.75 percent margin. If the margin is reduced to 2.5 percent, then the lender will receive $250 less per year as long as $100,000 is outstanding. If the loan is in place for ten years, the lender will lose $2,500.

In exchange for a margin that is lower by .25 percent, a buyer might pay an additional point, or $1,000 in the case of a $100,000 loan. Trading $1,000 for $2,500 may seem like a good deal, but there are three drawbacks.

First, if the mortgage is outstanding less than ten years, the lender's loss is less than $2,500.

Second, $1,000 is worth $2,593.74 over ten years if it's invested at 10 percent interest.

Third, most first-time buyers simply don't have a spare $1,000 up front, even if an opportunity to lower margin levels develops.

While trading points for better margin may be rare, an exchange for lower start rates is not.

POINTS, START RATES, AND CAPS

While lenders usually package ARMs so that margins are not negotiable, start rates are often elastic. Add points and start rates shrink, shrinkage that can hide a valuable benefit.

Suppose a 1-year ARM has a 9 percent start rate with 1 point. With 1.5 points, the start rate can drop three-eighths of a percent (.375) to 8.625 percent (9 percent less .375 equals 8.625 percent). If we pay 2 points up front, the start rate might be reduced to 8.25 percent, another three-eighths drops.

If we trade three-eighths of a percent off the starting interest rate by paying an extra half point up front, the economics work this way: For a $100,000 loan we are paying an additional $500 up front. Over a one-year period at 10 percent interest, $500 is worth $550. The value of three-eighths of a percent is just $375.

Although trading $550 for $375 may not seem attractive, a lower start rate offers two benefits.

First, if there is an annual cap, it means the maximum rate level in the second year, the third year, and so on is also reduced until we hit the lifetime cap.

Second, low start rates can also create a lower lifetime cap. For instance, if the start rate is 8 percent and a loan has a 4 percent lifetime cap, than the highest interest rate will be 12 percent. If the start rate is 7.5 percent, then the highest rate will be limited to 11.5 percent.

In considering more points for lower start rates, first-time buyers should be certain that the loan's maximum interest rate is also reduced. A lower cost up front, coupled with a lower lifetime cap, can make points more appealing, especially if seller "contributions" are available to offset buyer costs.

CONVERTIBLE ARMS

By any standard, ARMs are a radical departure from the dull, dependable fixed-rate loan, a departure that troubles many prospective homebuyers. To quell borrower worries, ARMs today often contain a conversion clause, a feature allowing borrowers to convert the loan to fixed-rate status.

The terms and conditions associated with such clauses vary from lender to lender, but in general such provisions work like this: With 30 days notice, the borrower may convert the outstanding loan balance to fixed-rate status at an interest rate equal to a particular index plus a .625 percent margin. The conversion fee typically ranges from $250 to $500.

Some lenders allow conversions once a year while others permit conversions at any time during the loan's first three to five years. As to rates, some cite an index plus a .625 percent margin rounded to the highest quarter. In effect, if an index is at 10.04 percent, the conversion rate will be 10.75 percent. (10.04 percent plus .625 percent equals 10.69 percent. Rounded to the highest quarter, the conversion rate is 10.75 percent.)

While conversion provisions soothe borrowers, there is some question as to whether they are particularly attractive. If rates go down, then ARM rates will also decline, lessening the desire to convert. Also, the addition of .625 percent or more to an index value will produce fixed interest levels that are higher than current ARM rates.

Since the cash required (usually $250 to $500) to convert is cheap, conversions may be more attractive than refinancing even when lower rates are available with a new loan. Refinancing will require more points, fees, charges, and taxes, money that might be better spent reducing loan balances.

But if it should ever happen that interest rates decline significantly, then conversion clauses can be very attractive, especially for those who intend to own their properties for many years.

7

Other Income Alternatives

While ARMs are among the most common and useful devices to stretch purchaser buying power, there are other approaches that also allow buyers with limited incomes to purchase first homes.

GRADUATED PAYMENT LOANS

ARMs are designed to entice borrowers with low initial rates and liberal qualification standards. Why not have a fixed-rate loan that offers the same values? There is such a loan product, what is known as a *graduated payment mortgage*, or GPM.

GPMs offer the stability of fixed-rate financing along with many terms similar to those which make ARMs so popular. To see how they work, consider a time when fixed-rate loans are priced at 10 percent interest.

If $100,000 is being borrowed over 30 years, a fixed-rate loan will require monthly payments of $877.57 for principal and interest. Add $150 a month for taxes and insurance, and PITI will equal $1,027.57. To qualify for this loan, a borrower will need at least a $44,000 income if 28/36 ratios are used.

With a GPM we can forget about initial payments of $877. Instead we can make the same loan but with far lower monthly costs up front. (See Table 27.)

The trick to a GPM is structure. A GPM has one interest rate but monthly payments that increase during the first five to ten years. With a five-year GPM, if we have a 7.5 percent yearly

Table 27   GRADUATED PAYMENT MORTGAGE VERSUS
                 CONVENTIONAL FINANCING

	GPM	Conventional
Loan Amount	$100,000	$100,000
Interest Rate	10 percent	10 percent
Monthly Payment		
Year 1	$667.04	$877.57
Year 2	$717.06	$877.57
Year 3	$770.84	$877.57
Year 4	$828.66	$877.57
Year 5	$890.81	$877.57
Years 6–30	$957.62	$877.57

payment increase and a 10 percent interest rate, our payments start at $667.04, rise for five years, and then in years 6 through 30 plateau at $957.62.

With that low start rate we no longer need a $44,000 income to qualify. Assuming that the qualifying rate and the start rate are the same, and again assuming $150 for taxes and insurance, we now need an annual income of $28,587.43 to qualify for this loan.

GPMs make great sense because rates are fixed and borrowers can qualify with little income. However, they do mask several problems that should concern first-time buyers.

First, because payment levels in the first years are low, GPMs commonly accumulate negative amortization.

Second, because GPMs feature negative amortization, they are a bad financing choice in areas where housing prices are stable or falling, or when buyers expect to own for only a short period of time.

Third, some GPMs do not have negative amortization. Instead, lenders offer low GPM payments up front if purchasers are willing to pay a "subsidy" fee at closing. In other words, there's no negative amortization because it is prepaid. If the *seller* pays some of your closing costs, GPMs with subsidy fees can be very attractive.

Fourth, some lenders will not qualify borrowers on the basis of the initial rate.

Fifth, some lenders qualify borrowers at the initial rate, but only if borrowers pay a lock-in fee. A *lock-in fee* is designed to assure that a given interest rate is available at closing, but by whatever name, a lock-in fee is a cash cost.

Is a GPM a good deal? A loan with fixed-rate graduated payments and liberal qualification standards should not be overlooked, especially by those who intend to own property for at least five years.

BOND-BACKED LOANS

The plight of first-time homebuyers is a major issue in many communities, not only because first-time buyers are a matter of general social concern, but also because first-time buyers often provide needed community services. Without affordable housing, the supply of workers declines, and when fewer workers are available in a community it is difficult to provide adequate public services or for businesses to find needed employees. Teachers, nurses, factory workers, computer programmers, secretaries, police officers, and firemen, among others, can only work in those areas where housing is available.

To assure that housing is available, many communities issue bond-backed or municipal mortgages. Because the issuing government—a state, city, or county—has better credit than most homebuyers, and because governments can assure debt repayments through taxation, they have little trouble issuing bonds that attract investor attention.

Since governments are good credit risks they normally pay less interest than you or I. In addition, the interest from such bonds is tax exempt, so investors have a far greater return than the stated interest rate.

Suppose the prevailing interest rate for ten-year corporate bonds is 10.5 percent. If a municipal bond offers 7 percent interest, it may not seem attractive until the tax implications are considered. An investor in such instruments is likely to be in the 33 percent federal tax bracket—the 28 percent bracket with a surcharge. In addition, the investor is also likely to face a state tax, perhaps 5 percent.

In this situation, if the investor buys corporate bonds his effective return is reduced by 38 percent (33 percent plus 5 percent). On bonds paying 10.5 percent, the after-tax rate is just 6.51

Table 28   BOND-BACKED MORTGAGES: A
SAMPLE

Corporate Bond Rate	10.5 percent
Effective Tax Rate	38.0 percent
Effective Bond Yield	6.51 percent
Bond-Backed Yield	7.00 percent
Borrower Rate	8.50 percent
Margin to Government	1.50 percent

percent. Suddenly municipal bonds look good, especially those backed by a local government's taxing authority.

The money raised from bond sales is made available to first-time homebuyers, typically those who have never bought a home or who have not owned real estate during the past three years.

The rates for such financing are usually set somewhat above the interest rate paid to investors, but well below rates charged by conventional lenders. If fixed-rate mortgages are available at 11 percent, municipal bonds can be priced at 8.5 percent. (See Table 28.)

Such pricing assures that the local government collects 8.5 percent interest for bonds on which it pays 7 percent to investors. The price differential covers administering the program as well as any expenses should borrowers default.

Municipal mortgages represent a good deal for first-time buyers as well. If a couple makes $45,000 a year, they will have $1,050 available each month for PITI if lenders allow a 28 percent front ratio. If taxes and insurance are $150 per month, then $900 is available for mortgage payments. At 11 percent interest a $900 payment can underwrite a mortgage worth $94,500. With 8.5 percent financing, the same couple can borrow $117,000.

Information about local bond-backed mortgages is available from governmental agencies and real estate brokers. In addition to ownership requirements, or a lack of them, such programs often have income caps relating to family size—the bigger the family, the bigger the income allowance.

8

Assumptions

New mortgages are not the only way to buy real estate. We can sometimes use existing financing by *assuming* the current owner's loan and his or her monthly payments. Sometimes we can even assume the old interest rate as well.

For example, suppose Conover wants to sell his home for $105,000. If Marzetti wants to buy the Conover house, and if Conover has a freely assumable $100,000 loan at 9 percent interest, then all Marzetti needs is a few thousand dollars to close the deal. With freely assumable financing in place, Marzetti need not worry about loan applications, changing interest rates, or points.

Assumable loans should be attractive to first-time buyers, but as a practical matter deals with such financing are often unworkable.

One problem is that freely assumable loans are a vanishing species, the snail darters of home financing. Virtually all freely assumable loans available today are older mortgages, some dating back to the 1960s and 1970s and carrying quaint interest rates of 6, 7, or 8 percent.

A second problem is that older loans may have small balances, so although they can be assumed, the value of such assumptions is limited.

Suppose a $75,000 loan was taken out 12 years ago by Mr. Sinclair. The loan is freely assumable and has an 8 percent interest rate. The financing is great, but what about the property? If the property is worth $150,000 today and the remaining loan balance is $70,000, then to buy this house a purchaser must come up with $80,000 in cash—or a combination of new financing and cash—to assume the old loan and to make the deal work.

Most loans made in recent years are *qualified assumptions,* financing where a loan may be assumed but only if the new borrower is approved by the lender. For loans with low fixed rates, it's possible that lenders will have exacting approval standards as well as many fees and charges. Less exacting, perhaps, are standards for ARMs, qualified assumptions where interest rates are forever current.

Still other loans are assumption hybrids. For example, FHA loans made before December 1, 1986, are freely assumable. Loans made after that date are qualified assumptions for 12 months. After one year has passed, FHA loans are then freely assumable by owner-occupants. Note that different rules apply for investors.

FHA loans can be particularly good assumption candidates because such financing requires less than 5 percent down. Find a home with an FHA loan that is two or three years old and the loan will be freely assumable. Because the loan is relatively young, and because only a small down payment was required up front, the difference between the sale price and the loan balance may be small, usually less than the 20 percent down required by conventional lenders.

VA loans made before March 1, 1988, are freely assumable, a mortgage pool that includes millions of loans. Because VA loans require no money down, remaining principal balances are often high and therefore, like FHA financing, the difference between the loan amount and the sale price is often small. VA loans made after March 1, 1988, are qualified assumptions.

9

Second Trusts

Assumable loans by themselves are often uninteresting when purchasers need huge amounts of cash to close a deal, as we saw with Mr. Sinclair's $75,000 mortgage in the last chapter.

But we can look at assumptions the way masons look at bricks: as something to build on.

With Mr. Sinclair we saw that he was selling a home for $150,000 and that the remaining loan balance was $70,000. Rather than bridge the gap between the sales price and the remaining loan balance with cash, why not get more financing?

If Sinclair or another source can lend us $65,000, we then have a deal that requires $15,000 down, or 10 percent of the sale price. Since the assumable $70,000 mortgage is a *first trust* or *first mortgage,* then a later loan will be will be called a *second trust* or *second mortgage.* There are technical differences between mortgages and trusts, but for our purposes, a loan is a loan. (See Table 29.)

There are sellers and lenders who make such deals, but rarely will they provide 90 percent financing. Usually borrowers must put down more than 10 percent to make the transaction work.

Lenders want buyers to make large down payments because seconds are risky and the lender's traditional enforcement tool, foreclosure, may be unworkable.

Imagine if Sinclair takes back a $65,000 second trust. Now the property secures financing worth $135,000—$70,000 for the first trust and $65,000 for the second.

Table 29   MR. SINCLAIR'S SECOND TRUST

Sale Price	$150,000	100.00 percent
Down Payment	$15,000	10.00 percent
First Trust Balance	$70,000	46.67 percent
Second Trust	$65,000	43.33 percent
First Trust Interest Rate		8 percent
Second Trust Interest Rate		11.5 percent
Combined Interest Rate		9.68 percent

If the borrower defaults on Sinclair's second trust, the property can be foreclosed. But if the property is put up for auction, any money collected will be used to pay taxes and then the first trust holder. Money left over, if any, will be used to satisfy Sinclair's claim.

If the property sells for $125,000 the payout might look like this: $3,000 for unpaid property taxes, $70,000 to the first-trust holder, and $52,000 to Sinclair. But Sinclair had a $65,000 note. What about the rest of his money, the other $13,000?

It may be possible to collect this money by suing the borrower, but then if the borrower had money it's unlikely that the property would have fallen into foreclosure. As a practical matter, Sinclair can say goodbye to his $13,000.

Second trusts may be used with assumable loans or in conjunction with new financing, but because such notes are more risky than first loans, it follows that they require higher interest rates. In Sinclair's case, the $70,000 first trust is available at 8 percent interest and we'll say that interest on the $65,000 second trust is set at 11.5 percent. The blended rate equals 9.68 percent.

Financing a home at 9.68 percent may not be a bad deal in a market where new financing is only available at 10 percent or higher. In addition, using a second trust rather than completely refinancing the property can lower closing costs for points and taxes.

Second trusts may give us access to assumable financing, but such loans are not without potential drawbacks. In addition to the higher interest rates mentioned earlier, second trusts are likely to feature either steep monthly payments or huge balloon notes.

BALLOON NOTES

In our example we saw how Sinclair created a $65,000 second trust with 11.5 percent interest. Paid out over 30 years, this loan will require monthly payments of $643.69. The only catch is that Sinclair, like most second trust lenders, doesn't want a 30-year note. He wants a five-year loan.

If Sinclair's note is paid in five years, the monthly payments will be enormous: $1,429.52 for the second trust plus payments on the first trust. The combined total payment for the first and second loans is so great that few people buying a $150,000 house could consider such exorbitant costs.

To make the loan palatable, second trusts are often set up so they have both a short-term (three to ten years) and a 30-year payout plan.

For Sinclair's second trust, the terms might include a $65,000 loan, interest at 11.5 percent, a five-year term, and monthly payments of $643.69.

Having greatly reduced monthly costs, we now run into another problem with Sinclair's loan. If the monthly payments are only $644, then the loan will not be repaid in five years. A large portion of the original debt remains outstanding, money that must be paid off in a single lump sum called a *balloon payment* when the loan ends. (See Table 30.)

With Sinclair's five-year note, the balloon payment will total $63,325.98—not much less than the original amount borrowed despite 60 payments of $643.69 and interest worth $48,751.11

Table 30   MR. SINCLAIR'S BALLOON NOTE OPTIONS

Loan Amount	$65,000	$65,000
Interest Rate	11.5 percent	11.5 percent
Loan Term	5 years	5 years
Payment Schedule	30 years	5 years
Monthly Payment	$643.69	$1,429.52
Balloon Payment	$63,325.96	0

over five years. Not a bad deal for Sinclair, or for any lender. Is a balloon note a good deal for borrowers?

When values are rising, a balloon note may allow us to purchase property when financing is otherwise not available and then sell or refinance before the lump sum is due.

If values are declining, or if financing is not available when the lump sum is due, then we have a problem. Money is owed but not payable, a situation that can result in foreclosure.

Not all second trusts are balloon notes, but many feature lump-sum payments. When considering a second trust, first-time buyers should ask if a balloon payment is due and, if so, how much. First-time buyers should also consider this thought: If monthly payments are low enough it's possible for the lump-sum payment to exceed the original debt!

WRAPAROUND MORTGAGES

The potential for large balloon payments makes second trusts an uncomfortable and unworkable form of financing for many first-time buyers. But what if we combined an assumable loan with a second trust of equal length?

We know that Sinclair has a freely assumable mortgage with a $70,000 balance. We also know the interest rate is 8 percent, that the monthly payments are $550.32, and that there are 18 years left on the 30-year note.

Rather than having a second trust, we can create a *wraparound loan* and work the deal like this:

- Sinclair will loan us $135,000.

- *Sinclair will continue to pay the $70,000 first trust.*

- The $135,000 loan will have an 18-year term.

- The $135,000 loan will be self-amortizing.

- Even though lenders are getting 10.5 percent interest for first trusts, let's say that Sinclair will loan us $135,000 at 10 percent interest. Sinclair, as we shall soon explain, can offer a lower rate because his actual return is far higher than the apparent interest level.

Here we have a situation where both seller and buyer benefit. We have avoided points and application costs associated with new financing while Sinclair has created a loan that will produce an attractive interest rate.

To see how much Sinclair is making, consider that he must continue to pay 8 percent interest on the $75,000 first trust, a $466.67 expense because some of the original principal has been paid down. Sinclair also receives $1,349.79 monthly for his 18-year, $135,000 loan. (See Table 31.)

The complicated question is this: How much does Sinclair make on his loan?

In the first month, he takes in $1,349.79, but part of this sum is amortization. His interest income is $1,125.

He must also make $466.67 monthly payments on the first trust. Some of this amount is amortization, but for our purposes it is an expense since the original loan must be repaid.

If we subtract $466.67 from $1,125 we can see that Sinclair earns $658.33 each month after expenses and amortization. Since we can calculate interest only on money actually loaned, $65,000 in this case, we can see that Sinclair makes 12.15 percent on his money, far more than the 10 percent face rate paid by a borrower.

Table 31   MR. SINCLAIR'S WRAPAROUND LOAN

Sale Price	$150,000
Amount Down	$15,000
Balance	$135,000
Wraparound Amount	$135,000
First Trust Balance	$70,000
Loan From Sinclair	$65,000
Wraparound Interest Rate	10.00 percent
Monthly Payment	$1,349.79
Monthly Interest	$1,125.00
Payment on First Trust	$466.67
Monthly Income	$658.33
Rate of Return	12.15 percent

Wraparound financing can be beneficial to both borrowers and lenders. In addition to sellers, commercial lenders will also be happy to make wraparound loans. Such loans, however, are complex and first-time buyers should only consider wraparound financing after consulting with a knowledgeable real estate attorney to assure that all terms and conditions are acceptable. In particular, buyers will want to make certain that the existing first trust payments are made in a timely manner by the wraparound lender; otherwise the property can be foreclosed.

10

Land Contracts

In some areas it's a common practice to finance real estate with what is known as a *land contract.* Also known as *contracts for deed, installment contracts,* and *conditional sale agreements,* such financing represents one of the worst deals for prospective first-time buyers.

To understand land contracts, imagine that you buy a refrigerator on credit. Each month you make payments, and when all the payments are made, the refrigerator is yours. But if you miss one or more payments, the appliance store sends a big truck and large employees to your home to take back its equipment. You lose your deposit and the value of all prior payments.

A land contract is very similar. You purchase a home and obtain land contract financing. You then make monthly payments to the lender and when the loan is paid off, or a certain portion is paid off, you finally get title to the property. Miss a payment and the lender can regain possession without a foreclosure.

Why no foreclosure? Because a land contract borrower does not have title and therefore there's nothing to foreclose. The lender already owns the property. The only issue is possession.

Land contracts raise sticky issues that should greatly trouble would-be buyers.

- If you make improvements to the property, who owns them?
- Who is responsible for repairs?

- Does the property come under any landlord/tenant regulations?

- Can you sell your rights under a land contract, or is transfer prohibited?

- If you have a home office, can it be depreciated since you do not have title to the property?

- Who deducts property tax payments?

- Can you refinance something you don't own?

Land contracts are often used in timeshare projects and recreational land sales, neither of which makes sense as a residential choice for first-time buyers. As for other forms of real estate, land contracts represent a financing concept so inherently unattractive that first-time buyers are well advised to avoid it altogether. If someone suggests a land contract, look elsewhere for financing.

11

Where to Find Financing

If there was a contest to determine the most popular business in America, mortgage lending could certainly compete. Just about everyone with cash, or access to someone else's cash, wants to be in the residential lending game, a fact one can easily confirm with a quick glance at the local phone book.

There are many lenders, and first-time buyers should feel free to call as many as possible. In addition to the phone book, lenders can also be found in newspaper real estate sections and by asking real estate lawyers, real estate brokers and agents, and people who have bought homes recently.

The best known lenders are often local savings and loan associations. Historically, S&Ls have collected deposits and then used their assets to provide mortgages for local borrowers. To this day S&Ls remain the largest source of residential mortgage financing.

In the past decade, however, many S&Ls (but not all) began making non-residential loans, mortgages for office buildings, shopping centers, and commercial projects. Such properties represent different economics and different risks when compared with home loans, and the results have been disastrous. Today the S&L business is shrinking as imprudent firms merge or go out of business.

The weeding process can be expected to continue for several years and the final result will be a strong S&L system that concentrates on loaning money to homebuyers. For first-time borrowers the important point is that S&Ls remain a major source of residential financing and if a local S&L has the best loan in town, grab it.

Commercial banks are another mortgage funding source, but unlike S&Ls, commercial banks are not primarily in the mortgage business. The mortgages banks offer are mostly available to business leaders who use, or might use, the bank's commercial services.

Both S&Ls and banks often provide real estate financing through mortgage loan subsidiaries. By using subsidiaries, lenders can operate outside their home jurisdictions and bring additional loan options to local borrowers.

Credit unions have provided first mortgages since 1978, and today they are a growing source of mortgage funds. Since members are typically known to credit unions on the basis of their work, credit unions may be in a unique position to assist first-time borrowers.

Insurance companies, with their huge capital reservoirs, are also major lenders. In the typical case, however, first-time buyers can obtain access to insurance funds only through mortgage bankers and mortgage brokers.

Mortgage bankers are individuals and organizations who loan their own funds and the funds of others to real estate purchasers. Once a mortgage is made, the mortgage banker typically sells the loan to an investor.

To understand how loans are sold, imagine that a mortgage banker has $1 million in capital. Five buyers come in, each gets a $200,000 mortgage, and now the banker's safe is empty—he has nothing left to loan.

To raise more money the banker takes his five loans, combines them into a "package," and sells the package to an investor, perhaps a pension fund or an insurance company. Once the loans are sold, the banker again has money to lend.

The banker makes money on the points, fees, and charges he is able to get from borrowers. He also may make a profit if the money market changes.

For example, if he has $200,000 fixed-rate loans at 10 percent interest and loan rates fall to 9.75 percent, the lender might be able to sell his loans for a premium price, something more than $200,000. If interest rates increase to 10.5 percent, then the face value for 9.75 percent loans will decline.

A banker can also make money by *servicing* loans—that is, by collecting payments from borrowers and then paying the money to investors, paying property taxes, and—if necessary—foreclosing.

A mortgage *broker,* unlike a mortgage *banker,* does not have capital to lend but instead loans money that belongs to others. He makes his money on fees, charges, and points. In addition, a mortgage broker may also service loans.

CONFORMING AND PORTFOLIO LOANS

We just saw how a local banker was able to take five loans, combine them in a package, and then sell the package to investors. S&Ls, credit unions, and mortgage bankers also package loans for resale.

Loan packages are sold in the *secondary market,* an electronic network that connects buyers and sellers around the country. Some of the biggest buyers in the secondary market include the Federal National Mortgage Association (Fannie Mae), the Federal Home Loan Mortgage Corporation (Freddie Mac), the Government National Mortgage Association (Ginnie Mae), insurance companies, and pension funds.

To make sure everyone knows what's for sale, packages sold in the secondary market contain *conforming loans*—loans that meet certain standards or guidelines. For example, ratios of 28/36 might be required for every loan that represents 90 percent financing. As another example, loan sizes may be limited to not more than $187,600.

While the secondary market enables local lenders to make more loans than might otherwise be possible, not all loans are destined for the secondary market. Some lenders, usually larger ones, offer *non-conforming* or *portfolio loans.*

 Portfolio loans can be extremely attractive because the standards and guidelines required in the secondary market can be ignored. Ratios can be more liberal and loan limits may be higher, factors that should encourage first-time buyers to ask every would-be lender if they make portfolio loans.

12

Questions for Lenders

Because there are so many mortgage formats and so many lenders, it follows that first-time borrowers will need a checklist to sort through locally available loans. Ask the right questions and it becomes possible to quickly separate good deals from less enticing choices.

Asking questions should not be seen as pushy or embarrassing. If you don't ask questions, if you don't know which questions to ask, then the probability of getting a good deal becomes minuscule. Speaking to many lenders is the best way not only to pinpoint a good deal, but also to learn about lending.

Besides, you're the consumer. *Lenders should compete for your business.* If they want your loan, let them prove they're offering the best possible deal.

To find a good lender, see who advertises in phone books and newspaper real estate sections. Also, speak to real estate brokers, attorneys, and those who have recently purchased homes.

If your basic list has three or four names, keep looking. Calling lenders may be time-consuming and boring, but the more lenders you call, the better your chances of getting a good deal, one that may save thousands of dollars.

Once your basic list is established, call each lender and ask for a loan officer who can provide information about residential mortgage programs. After explaining that you want information about *owner-occupant* housing, here's what to ask:

- What rate and points are you charging today for 30-year fixed-rate financing with 20 percent down? Since a fixed-rate conventional loan is offered by most lenders, this information can serve as a basic point of comparison.

- Do you also have fixed-rate loans with 10 percent down? If so, what are the rates and points?

- What is your lowest down payment requirement with fixed-rate financing?

- If I put down less than 20 percent, do you require private mortgage insurance? If so, for a loan of $_____, what is the cost for PMI at closing and what is the cost each month? If you offer lump-sum PMI, how much will it cost and can the premium be added to the loan amount?

- If I pay an additional point, how much will the fixed rate decline?

How To Have a Stronger Loan Application

1. Check your credit with a credit reporting agency. Correct errors, update information, note any items in dispute.

2. If possible, defer the start of a new job until after settlement.

3. Have basic loan information up to date, assembled, and available to a loan officer at the time of application. See Chapter 13 for a list of typical items.

4. Once application has been made, tell the loan officer you expect a weekly progress update. If you don't hear from the loan officer on a regular basis, feel free to call. Ask if the loan has gone to underwriting, if underwriting has approved the loan, and if you can pick up a written confirmation that the loan has been approved. After you get written confirmation, send copies to the seller or the seller's broker, as appropriate.

5. If the loan has yet to be approved, ask if more information and documentation are required. Respond as quickly as possible to speed the application process.

- If I pay one point less, how much will the fixed rate increase?
- What are your front and back ratios for 80 percent LTV financing?
- What are your front and back ratios for 90 percent LTV financing?
- What are your front and back ratios for 95 percent LTV financing?
- Do you offer VA and FHA loans? If so, what are your current rates and points for each program?
- If we receive a gift from a parent or relative, do you require a gift letter? Is there any other documentation required for a gift? Is there a minimum cash amount we must put up even if we get a gift?

Each lender is likely to have several ARM programs. Here are the major points to consider:

- Will you please compare your six-month ARM, one-year ARM, and three-year ARM programs?
- What index is used with each program?
- What margin is used with each program?
- Is there a *payment cap* for each program? If so, how much?
- What is the *yearly interest cap* for each program?
- What is the *lifetime interest cap* for each program?
- What is the start rate and how long does it last?
- Is the lifetime cap, say 4 percent or whatever figure, based on the start rate or another figure?
- Do you qualify ARM borrowers with the start rate, or with a different rate?
- If you qualify ARM borrowers with a qualifying rate that differs from the start rate, what is the qualifying rate you use?
- How many points are required for each ARM program?
- If I pay more points, what happens to the start rate?
- If I pay fewer points, what happens to the start rate?

- To obtain the rates quoted, must I pay a lock-in fee? If so, how much? (If a loan is locked in, then a borrower is guaranteed a certain rate.)

- If I pay a lock-in fee, how long is the lock-in period? Exactly when does the lock-in period begin and when does it end?

- Does the lock-in agreement include both rates *and* points? (If a lock-in agreement says a loan will be made at 10 percent but is silent on points, by closing the rate may be unchanged while the lender's requirement for points increases dramatically. A lock-in that says nothing about points is potentially worthless.)

- If you are offering a graduated payment mortgage, must I pay a "subsidy" fee at closing to get the best available rate? If so, how much?

- Can you provide a buyer qualification letter? (Buyer qualification letters typically state that a purchaser is able to qualify for a specific amount of financing at a particular rate and terms. Such letters are invariably couched in language saying the lender's opinion is not binding and depends on verification of the purchaser's income and debts as well as a property appraisal.)

- How much do you charge to process a loan application?

- Do you offer a pre-qualification program? If so, what is the cost to participate? Assuming an adequate appraisal, does the pre-qualification program guarantee both rates and points? When will the rates and terms available under a pre-qualification program expire?

13

Pre-Qualification Programs

During the past few years, lenders have made strenuous efforts to reduce the processing time required for individual home loans. There are now pre-qualification programs and even 15-minute mortgages, loan concepts that can be valuable to first-time buyers.

Pre-qualification programs resolve many application hassles, clearly show how much you can afford, and strengthen purchaser bargaining power.

Consider what happens if a seller receives two offers, each for $125,000. Both prospective buyers seem qualified but one produces a prequalification certificate from a lender showing that he or she is qualified to borrow $115,000 with 90 percent financing. Rather than wait 45 to 60 days to find out if the second purchaser also qualifies, the seller naturally prefers the buyer with a mortgage commitment in hand.

In reviewing pre-application programs, borrowers should understand that not all programs offer the same benefits. Some pre-qualification programs merely estimate how much borrowers can afford while others represent actual loan commitments.

Programs that *guarantee* financing are nothing more than fast-track processing plans with minimum documentation. To participate in a typical program you must complete a standard loan application and present needed documentation at the time of application. Documents to bring include:

- W-2 forms for the past two years.

- Tax returns for the past two years for those who are self-employed, participate in partnerships, or own 25 percent or more of a corporation.

- Your three most recent pay stubs (originals, not copies).

- Your three most recent checking, savings, and investment account statements (originals, not copies).

- Form DD-212 if you are applying for VA-backed funding.

- A balance sheet and year-to-date profit and loss statement if you are self-employed. Be aware that some quickie loan programs may not accept applications from self-employed individuals because it can be difficult to verify current income.

- The name and relationship of any donor if you are purchasing with a gift.

The trick to pre-qualification programs is not that the documentation is different from normal lender requirements, but instead that borrowers present their documentation *at the time of application* rather than sending it in over several weeks. Pre-qualification programs are a tangible benefit to those who assemble needed loan documents before making a loan application.

Once the materials are delivered, the lender will take three to four days to review your credit history. If everything is in order, you will then receive a detailed loan commitment that may be good for 30, 60, or 90 days. The commitment will show (or should show) how much you can borrow at given rates and points. Some lenders automatically qualify applicants for both fixed-rate and adjustable-rate financing, a comparison which typically shows that ARMs create far more borrowing power than fixed-rate loans.

Although many pre-qualification programs can be used to obtain loan commitments, first-time buyers should understand that such commitments are not absolute. A lender must be satisfied that the property has sufficient market value before a loan can be issued. In addition, as a closing condition, a lender is also likely to demand a survey. If either the appraisal or survey are unsatisfactory, lenders may "decline" the loan.

In considering pre-qualification programs, first-time buyers should ask lenders these questions:

- Does your program merely estimate my ability to borrow or is it a firm commitment to lend money?

- If it's a firm commitment, when does the commitment begin and when does it end?

- Is the commitment for both rates and points, or just for interest rates? Without a points commitment, it's possible for the rate to remain unchanged while the required number of points soars by closing.

- What is the cost to apply for this program? Will the fee be regarded as a credit at closing?

While pre-qualification programs should be seen as desirable and advantageous, they are not a substitute for the best rates and terms available. A speedy program with higher interest rates is not a bargain.

Pre-qualification programs are designed for those who intend to purchase property in the near future, but they can *sometimes* have another use as well. If you need a quick loan commitment, some lenders may allow you to apply for financing with a pre-qualification program, a strategy that can result in faster loan processing and earlier settlements.

THE 15-MINUTE ILLUSION

If you've got time for a coffee break, you've got time for a mortgage, or at least that's what many lenders seem to be saying as they promote 15-minute loan programs. Fill out an application, wait for a computer to whiz and hum, and 15 minutes later you can have a complete mortgage program, subject only to a satisfactory property appraisal and survey.

Any effort to speed the loan application process should be wildly applauded, but unfortunately some programs are unlikely to offer much help to first-time buyers. Fast approval programs that require 20 percent down effectively eliminate speedy processing for those who finance with FHA, VA, and bond-backed mortgages. Happily, quickie loan programs with as little as 10 percent down are becoming more common, and it is the programs with small down payment requirements that are most likely to help first-time buyers.

Although 15-minute programs hold an undeniable attraction, first-time borrowers should be aware that while convenience is attractive, convenience may also be costly.

If a quickie loan for $100,000 costs just .50 percent more than one from a lender who offers 10 percent financing but longer processing, it means the speedy loan will require an additional $37.17 per month as long as the loan is outstanding. Over five years, the quickie application will require additional payments worth $2,230.

Once a speedy loan is approved, you then have enough time to shop for lower rates and better terms. If no better deal is available, you can always fall back on the 15-minute mortgage.

Going with another lender may mean that your loan application fee for the 15-minute mortgage will be lost. But if a change in lenders results in better rates and terms, the benefits should greatly outweigh any application fee.

LOCK-INS

When considering various loan programs, it's important to understand that a lender's *quoted rates do not necessarily reflect a firm commitment* to provide a loan at a given rate and terms.

The mortgage market changes each day and with each change there are new rates. For instance, if your application is in by a given time, say 11 A.M., then you may be able to lock in the particular rate and terms quoted during the past 24 hours. If your application is received after 11 A.M., then new rates and terms may apply.

Lenders typically have three lock-in policies. In some cases, loans are locked in at the time of application and the rate and terms quoted are the rate and terms you receive.

Other lenders only lock in rates once applications have been approved. If it takes four weeks to review a loan application, then the rates and terms in place a month later—whether higher or lower—are yours.

A third approach is no lock-in. Your rate and terms are determined at the time of settlement, an approach that offers no security at all.

First-time buyers should ask about lock-in policies, not only when rates are locked in but whether points and all other terms are locked in as well. If rates are guaranteed but not points, it's then possible that rates will remain unchanged but points will rise.

Also, beware of lock-in forms that are not absolute. A lock-in form that gives a lender the right to change rates and terms for any reason is a sham. Ask to see the lender's standard lock-in certificate at the time you apply for a loan and be sure it represents a firm commitment. Be sure also that the lock-in form you see and the one you receive are identical.

Some lenders allow (or require) borrowers to pay lock-in fees to assure particular rates and terms. If you pay a lock-in fee, be certain that both rates and points are guaranteed. Also, be sure the lock-in period is long enough, at least 60 days from application. If the lock-in period is shorter and closing is delayed, then the lock-in can expire and the lock-in fee will be lost.

14

How to Find the Right Community

Every first-time buyer wants the best possible home, a goal closely related to finding the best possible community. Communities are important because the value and potential of any property can be reduced or destroyed by the surrounding area. Pick the wrong area and houses that seem cheap today may become expensive tomorrow if they do not appreciate at the same rate as other nearby properties.

To see how this works, consider two communities. In Southwick homes are priced at $100,000 and values increase at 6 percent yearly. Northwick homes cost $110,000 today but values are increasing by 8 percent annually.

It may appear that a Southwick property is the better deal. It's less expensive, needs less money down, and requires smaller monthly payments. The Northwick property may be appreciating faster, but is 2 percent such a big deal? You bet.

Today the gap between properties in these two communities is $10,000, but in five years the gap will widen. In approximate terms, a home in Southwick will be worth $133,825 while one in Northwick will command prices of $161,625—a $27,800 difference. In 10 years the difference will be even more pronounced, $179,000 to $237,500.

The difference in values over time is not merely a statistical oddity. The Northwick owner will have more equity and thus more ability to borrow. If owners in each community sell after

10 years, the Northwick owner will pocket an additional $58,500 to underwrite a new home.

It should be pointed out, however, that the entire $58,500 is not excess value since the Northwick owner paid an additional $10,000 to acquire his home originally.

As much as we want a home that reflects our tastes, values, and preferences, we also want a property that represents a good investment. Since we are unlikely to live in a first home for many years, economic potential may be a more important issue than style or status.

A home thus represents not only an investment in real estate, but also an investment in a local community. And while we may like a given neighborhood, self-interest cannot be ignored. If values are rising faster in one area than another, then as a matter of economic self-interest we must at least consider the neighborhood that offers the most growth potential.

Our goal is not to buy in areas where prices are now steep, but to purchase where they will be steep tomorrow. If we can anticipate demand, if we can project future growth, then the money we spend on housing can produce additional value.

SPOTTING GROWTH

Every community has neighborhoods where values are rising faster than others, and to find them we need to look for markers suggesting future growth and development.

Local pricing trends are certainly one index of demand, an index that should be considered with care.

Rising prices suggest demand, and strong demand will mean that bargains are rare. But if a given neighborhood is a marketing hot spot, what about areas nearby? Once today's hot neighborhood is developed, improved, filled in, and gentrified, what area will be next? *It's the next area that offers the best opportunity for future growth, the place where current buyers can make the largest profit.*

Why will areas grow tomorrow? Look for objective reasons such as new roads, office construction, malls, and schools. Search for expanding hospitals, new factories, streets that need to be widened and bridges that must be replaced.

Some of the information we need may be visible from the street while other data will come from local newspapers. We should also check with local government offices that specialize in planning, zoning, and economic development, offices that track local trends. The experts in such offices should be able to provide maps, population and employment projections for the next five to ten years, and a prospectus or "official statement" from recent bond issues. Bond issues often contain valuable information showing how local communities envision their growth.

Look also at local housing. In areas where growth is antici-pated we should see that new homes are under construction, that older homes are being refurbished, and that prices for finished building lots are rising.

EXPLORING COMMUNITIES

Once developmental trends have been established, the next step is to consider areas that seem promising.

We want to see how neighborhoods look today and project how they may evolve five to ten years from now, an educational process that will take time and study.

Weekends should be set aside to visit different communities. We want to stop by stores and shops, visit real estate brokers, and also see area homes. Because new houses are typically open both Saturday and Sunday, we want to visit them on Saturdays. Exist-ing homes are usually held open on Sunday afternoons, so Sun-days should be set aside for re-sale properties.

There are basic questions we want to ask for each neighbor-hood or community we consider:

- What proportion of local residents work within the commu-nity?

- What schools are available within the community, both public and private?

- Are there religious institutions and congregations of interest to us in the community?

- What community improvements are planned or under con-struction? How will they be funded?

- What recreational facilities are now available, facilities such as parks, tennis courts, golf courses, and swimming centers?

- Are private recreational facilities available? If so, at what cost? How does one join?

- What day care facilities are available?

- Are there area medical facilities such as hospitals, emergency clinics, and private offices for physicians, dentists, and optometrists?

- Is area activity seasonal, such as a summer beach resort or a winter ski center? If so, what facilities are open during the off season?

Have property taxes risen during the past two years? If not, are tax increases anticipated in the near future? Be aware that in many jurisdictions property taxes rise even when rates remain stable. This is possible because rates are tied to property values, say $1.25 in taxes per $1,000 in value. As property values increase, taxes go up automatically even though rates remain constant.

How much does it cost to rent? When asking about rentals, compare similar units—that is, three-bedroom townhouses with three-bedroom townhouses. Otherwise, rent levels can be misleading.

In asking these questions and similar ones, buyers should be aware that even with the best plans and projections, areas which seem ripe for growth sometimes stagnate. *There are no guarantees that neighborhoods will grow, that values will rise, or that demand will continue.* Beware of folks who tell you differently.

THE COMMUTING GAME

In many urban and suburban areas commuting has emerged as a major headache for first-time buyers. To acquire more affordable housing, first-time purchasers are often forced to buy where land is less expensive, land that may be 29 miles from downtown.

The result is a situation where first-time buyers substitute higher housing costs for more expensive commuting, expenses that include larger gasoline and insurance bills and perhaps the need for an additional car.

Productive time, or the loss of productive time, is another commuting expense. Commute one hour twice daily and you lose two hours a day, 10 hours a week, 520 hours a year—the equivalent of 13 work weeks! Time spent in transit is time lost to friends, family, leisure, and the workplace.

To complicate matters further, commuting has emerged as the great national lie.

Ask someone how long it takes to get downtown or to another central location, and the answer may well be "20 minutes." This answer is absolutely true—at midnight, if there are no roadway accidents, no trains have derailed, and nothing is under construction. Conversely, if your schedule requires you to be on the road at more popular times, say Tuesday mornings at 8 A.M., then wide-open spaces, high speeds, and fast commuting times are likely to evaporate.

In most major cities rush hours are getting longer and commuting consumes more time. Worse, the future looks bleak. Studies in many areas show that average speeds for major arterial roads are expected to decline significantly in coming years.

With thoughts of rush-hour madness in mind, it makes sense to rise early, travel to neighborhoods where you may one day live, and then commute with everyone else for several mornings. This may be inconvenient, but it may also be an eye-opening experience.

STATISTICAL GAMES

Prospective buyers will want to know something about area pricing levels, but with the understanding that general pricing patterns are often difficult to interpret.

You may hear that prices "rose 14 percent in the past year," a statement that at one and the same time is perhaps both correct and useless. It is possible that a year ago four townhouses sold for an average price of $100,000 and that this year one single-family house has been marketed for $114,000. Since townhouses and single-family homes are different commodities, the average price figure does not tell us whether values have risen, fallen, or remained constant.

To find "average" sale prices we take the total dollar volume of all area sales during a given period and divide that figure by the number of homes sold. In a one-year period we might have $58 million in total sales representing 512 transactions, or an average price of $113,281.

Average prices do not tell us what was sold. If our 512 properties include 400 townhouses at $100,000 each and 112 single-family homes at $160,714 each, then the average price is too high for townhouses and too low for single-family homes. To be realistic, we need to compare townhouses with townhouses and single-family homes with single-family homes.

We also need to look at sale volume. An increase in volume coupled with rising prices suggests increased demand. A decrease in sale volume along with steady or falling prices indicates a drop in demand.

While general pricing patterns are often less than objective, they are important. If prices are perceived as rising, seller expectations will rise and it will be hard for first-time buyers to bargain. If prices are seen as stagnant or headed down, then good deals may abound as sellers rush to unload their properties.

15

The Search for a Swan

We often see real estate as a mythic ideal. Architectural magazines show us the latest styles while on television we can view the homes of the rich, the famous, and the excessive. Beautiful homes can be found in every community, the very homes we would love to own.

Yet homeownership and homebuying are different. We want to own the best possible house, but as first-time buyers we know that a beautiful property, a home that is well maintained, newly painted, and perfectly decorated, is also a home that can be sold at the highest possible price.

We want a home that has not been painted in recent years because we know that paint is inexpensive and we can do it ourselves. We want a house where weeds are plentiful and grass is knee-high because we know that gardening is cheap and easy. We want a home that reflects the worst possible decor because when the owners move, their furnishings move with them. We want a house where the basement and garage are clogged with boxes and debris, stuff that will either go with the owners or that can be thrown out.

What we really want is a property that is well located, properly sized, and structurally sound, but at the same time looks like a candidate for urban renewal. We want a house that has been on the market for many weeks because it shows poorly, a property that is not in demand, and—because it's not in demand—a house that will not command a steep purchase price.

We don't want to purchase a shell that requires major renovations, but we do want a house that will allow us to capture excess value because we know that as first-time buyers the best way to acquire a home is to trade labor for condition, to buy property that has the potential to increase in value if someone will merely take the time and make the effort to paint it, clean it, and fix it.

As buyers we want a home that is ugly today, but capable of being beautiful tomorrow. We want a swan.

HOW TO PRICE REAL ESTATE

How much should you pay for a given property? That is the one question confronted by all first-time buyers, a question which cannot be ignored, hidden, or delayed. Answer wrong and you pay for years.

Housing values are certainly influenced by supply and demand. The more something is in demand, the higher the price. And it's true, as the real estate industry reminds us, that the supply of land is frozen, that no more is being made.

But supply is not a problem in this country, at least not in an immediate sense. Fly from Washington to Los Angeles or San Francisco and you can see vast stretches of open land, much of which appears unoccupied or at least underutilized. If what you want is land, follow Horace Greeley's advice and go west.

The real issue is that there are few places where we want to live. We want to be near jobs, culture, convenience, and recreation, a combination that largely identifies the cities and suburbs where we now reside and where we want to buy.

PRICING GUIDELINES

Finding the right price for a given property is not a science, but at least there are certain guidelines and observations we can use to make informed judgments.

First, a property's selling price is determined at one point in time under specific conditions through the agreement of a buyer and seller. Property values may be different at any other point in time, with any other conditions, or with different buyers or sellers.

Second, interest rates and prices are inversely related. As

rates go up, prices fall. Suppose the Warren home is priced at $100,000 when interest rates are at 9.5 percent. With 10 percent down, a $90,000 mortgage will require monthly payments of $756.77. If interest rates rise to 10 percent, the same monthly payment will only underwrite a $86,234.42 loan. To create a workable deal with higher interest rates, either the buyer must pay more per month to obtain a $90,000 loan, or the seller's price must be reduced, or both buyer and seller must compromise.

Third, first-time buyers, and all purchasers, want the least expensive home in the most expensive neighborhood they can afford. This is a basic rule in real estate, one explained by common preferences and common sense. No one wants to pay $200,000 to live in a neighborhood where homes typically cost $100,000, even if $200,000 buys the best house. For the higher figure, buyers can get the benefits of a neighborhood with $200,000 houses.

Conversely, if you can buy a $75,000 property in a neighborhood where $100,000 properties are common, you may have a bargain. If it takes $10,000 in repairs, painting, and improvements to bring the property up to neighborhood standards, then you have captured *extra value* worth $15,000 in this case ($75,000 plus $10,000 equals $85,000. If the neighborhood supports $100,000 prices, the buyer is ahead by $15,000).

Fourth, real estate is worth no more than the amount someone is willing to pay. The fact that a house is offered for sale at a given price means only that the seller has identified a starting point in the bargaining process.

Fifth, real estate cannot be sold for less than a seller is willing to take. A buyer must offer enough to make a sale worthwhile, otherwise a seller will hold the property for personal use or rent it.

Sixth, every real estate deal mixes both money and terms. The usual trade is money for terms; pay more and get better terms, pay less and terms are reduced. For example, Truitt's property can be sold for $150,000 if he spends $5,000 to fix the roof. It might also be sold for $145,000 to a buyer willing make needed repairs.

Seventh, selling times and selling prices are inversely related. The longer a home is on the market, the more likely the sale price will decline.

THREE METHODS OF PRICING

Within real estate there are three generally recognized home pricing methods.

The first approach is to base property values on the income that can be produced. The income system is most appropriate for commercial real estate and for use by investors.

A second approach looks at replacement values. If a property burned to the ground tomorrow, how much will it cost to replace all the wood, bricks, lumber, plumbing, electrical, and other building components? What about labor, permits, design costs, etc.? This type of analysis is complex and typically used to value unique structures such as schools, churches, synagogues, and town halls.

The pricing system offering the most promise for first-time buyers is the *market data approach,* which simply compares recent sales among similar homes *in the same area.* If someone says a property is worth $125,000 because like homes four miles away are selling for that price, the comparison may be useless. What about homes on the next block or around the corner?

Although similar homes are likely to share many features, they are not identical. Even houses on the same block and built by the same developer will be different.

The central point is not that homes are different, but that some differences are more important to us than others. Our individual needs, goals, and perceptions will form the grading system used to evaluate each property we see. Table 32 as well as the list below illustrate basic features to consider.

Amenities. Amenities are the extras that come with a house, benefits that may not be necessary but add much to the property. Amenities include such items as fireplaces, skylights, and decks.

Attics. There was a time when attics could be used for storage or even additional living space. Today, however, attic advantages are often limited by modern construction techniques. When forms shaped like a huge "W" are placed every 16 inches and used to support the roof, the attic below does not have clear space that can be used efficiently.

Table 32　HOMEBUYER COMPARISON CHART

	House #1	House #2	House #3
Address Price Broker Broker's Phone Number			
Number of Bedrooms Number of Full Baths Number of Half Baths Number of Quarter Baths			
Kitchens Eat-In Galley Country			
Amenities Fireplace Skylights Decks Storm Doors Storm Windows Clothes Washer Clothes Dryer Dish Washer Disposal Pantry Shelving Built-In Cabinets Carpeting Wooden Floors			
Attic No Storage Some Storage Possible Living Space			

Table 32 (*Continued*)

	House #1	*House #2*	*House #3*
Basement Crawl Space Full Size Finished Walk-Out Dry Light			
Construction Wood Frame Aluminum Siding Brick CBS Brick and Frame Other			
Ownership Fee Simple Condo Co-op Monthly Fee			
Style Detached Attached Townhouse Apartment-Style Flat			
Grounds Lot Size Trees Flat Fenced Landscaping			

Table 32 (*Continued*)

	House #1	*House #2*	*House #3*
Utilities Heat Air-Conditioning Hot Water Public Water? Public Sewage? Monthly Utilities Expenses			
Garage Off-Street Parking			
Other Features Schools Shopping Religious Facilities Public Transportation Playgrounds Day Care Distance to Fire Hydrant			

Basements. In those areas where basements are common, there are few home features that represent as much potential value. A *dry,* well-lighted basement can add 50 percent more living area to a two-story home, 100 percent to a single-story ranch house.

Built-Ins. Many homes are particularly attractive because shelves, dining room cabinets, pantries, and other items have been built in and attached to the property. Built-in items generally convey with the property, a pleasant bonus in many cases.

Configuration. The issue here is traffic flow. Dining rooms should be adjacent to kitchens, kitchens should have exterior entrances, and bedrooms should be widely spaced.

Construction. We need to know if a house is brick, CBS (concrete, brick, and stucco), wood frame, brick and frame, frame with aluminum siding, brick with aluminum siding, stone, log, etc.

The "best" construction is a matter of taste. For example, wood frame is attractive but brick does not require painting. Then again, older brick homes may need to be "re-pointed," an expensive process to replace missing mortar.

When evaluating different construction materials and techniques, first-time buyers should ask if the property has been well maintained, and whether costly repairs will be needed shortly.

Fees.   How much are condo or co-op fees, if anything? Because condo and co-op fees cover different costs, comparisons are often difficult. For instance, co-op fees typically include payments for an underlying mortgage while condo fees do not.

Fire Hydrants.   We want fire hydrants, and we want them near our property. The reason? Property insurance is cheaper if our property is close to a hydrant, say within 600 feet or less.

Floors.   While the purpose of floors has remained stagnant for many centuries, flooring choices have evolved. Today, buyers will find that hardwood, carpet, tile, and linoleum flooring are all available, often in the same property.

A proper hardwood or tile floor can literally last a lifetime, while other flooring materials substitute a lower initial cost for shorter life spans. Look for flooring that is attractive, easy to maintain, and will last throughout your intended span of ownership.

Fuel.   How is the property heated and air-conditioned? What type of fuel does the stove require? The hot water heater? Since fuel costs vary around the country, choosing the wrong fuel supply can be a significant expense, one that is not easy to reduce.

We need to know how much the seller pays each year for fuel costs, but with the understanding that a given fuel bill may not relate to our situation. For instance, if the sellers have eight children and run 30 laundries each week, their fuel costs to heat water and power appliances will be far larger than the fuel bill faced by a smaller family.

Kitchens.   A kitchen is arguably the most important single area in a home. Kitchens can be utterly plain and utilitarian, but increasingly they are social centers where people congregate even when meals are not being served. A growing trend links kitchens, living rooms, and dining rooms to form a social and entertainment hub known as a "great room."

Food preparation areas can be described as "galley kitchens" (a small isle surrounded by cabinets and appliances), "eat-in kitchens" (kitchens containing space for eating), and "country kitchens," which offer expansive areas for cooking and eating.

Lot Size.   Buying a home implies land ownership, though this may not be the case with an apartment-style condo or co-op. Having a large lot is not necessarily our goal, especially if mowing, raking, and gardening are not regarded as pleasant, restful chores. Instead we want enough land to assure privacy, but not so much that we are engulfed in maintenance and upkeep.

Parking.   A place to park one or more cars is critically important in downtown areas and extremely convenient in the suburbs. Attached garages are the best parking alternative because they potentially represent additional living space when insulated and finished.

Proximity.   Real estate markets are extremely localized, and in some cases values on one block may not apply to properties across the street or down the road. Homes of equal size but in neighboring subdivisions commonly have different values. Even within the same building, condo units often have different values depending on their location—more for a top unit, less for a unit by the dumpster, more for a beachfront unit, less for a unit facing the road.

Proximity is often hard to grasp. The owner who says, "My house would be worth $400,000 if it was located in Jasper Hills" misses the point. His or her property is not in Jasper Hills, it's elsewhere, and values elsewhere are different.

Buyers, too, often have trouble with proximity. Those who move to Boston, Los Angeles, San Francisco, or New York from less expensive areas are often amazed by the prices they find.

Such purchasers sometimes remark, "Gee, back home I had a four-bedroom house. For the same money all I can buy here is a measly townhouse 20 miles from downtown." Back home, as well, they probably didn't have the economic opportunities which underlie high prices.

Public Water and Sewer.   Does the property have public water and sewer? If not, is there a well on the property? A septic tank? We also want to know how much the seller pays for water each year.

Size.   Size is critical when evaluating property values. We want to know how much land is being sold and we also want to know how many square feet are in the house. Unfortunately, home interiors often produce a surprising array of measurements. When determining size, some owners and builders measure wall to wall while others omit garage space, balconies, and unfinished basement areas to give a better picture. When told that a property has "1,500 square feet of living space" always ask how "living space" is defined and what's included and excluded.

Another approach to size is to count bedrooms and bathrooms. A bedroom can be defined as any *private* space large enough for a bed and dresser. As to bathrooms, they are generally described as full (a sink, bath or shower, and toilet), half (sink and toilet), or quarter (toilet).

In our modern era the old standards for bedrooms and baths are in disarray. Many properties today, even townhouses, feature "a master bedroom suite plus two additional bedrooms and a central bath." This redundant description tells us that the property has, at least, a combination bedroom and bathroom, two additional bedrooms, and a bathroom shared by residents of the two additional bedrooms. A "master bedroom" is thus something more than a simple place to sleep.

Bathrooms have also changed. A bathroom may now include a whirlpool bath, a walk-in shower, a steam room, multiple sinks, a towel closet, extensive cabinetry, sun lamps, as well as decorator tile and wallpaper. In the comparison process, a facility with more features than a health spa deserves a higher ranking than a full bath.

Storm Windows and Doors.   Homes with storm windows and doors are cheaper to heat and cool. In addition, they reduce maintenance costs by shielding windows and doors from direct contact with rain, snow, and ice. If storm windows and doors are already installed, that is one less expense faced by prospective buyers.

Style.   Is the property detached or attached? Is it a Cape Cod, ranch, colonial, bi-level, or split level?

Taxes.   We want to know what the current owners pay each year for property taxes. This cost is likely to rise if we buy because a new and higher value will be recorded for the property. Also, what is included in the tax bill? Some jurisdictions bill separately for garbage collection and other services.

Special Features.   Does the property have special features such as a porch, deck, microwave oven, clothes washer and clothes dryer, one or more fireplaces, hardwood floors, carpeting, a pool, or modifications for the handicapped such as ramps and wide doors?

TRADING OFF: A CHECKLIST

Go from house to house and it will become apparent that each local housing market offers a surprising number of property choices. There are homes of every size, design, and location, a surplus of alternatives in a world dominated by a shortage of cash and credit.

For first-time buyers the cruel reality is that unless you have vaulted into the upper brackets, much of the housing market is effectively off limits. There may be many features the ideal house should contain, but the ideal house is also likely to be unafford-able.

More likely by far are imperfect homes; homes with some good features, but homes that also lack something. In such an environment prospective buyers must ask: What is important to me? What can I live without? Before looking at individual homes, consider the questions raised here.

The questions raised in the "Purchaser's Checklist" reflect a

The Purchaser's Checklist

How much money do I have at this time for a down payment and closing costs? _____.

Can I buy alone, or am I willing to purchase with others? _____.

How can I spend less and earn more? _____.

How many miles am I willing to commute? _____.

How much time am I willing to spend in traffic? _____.

What is the minimum number of bedrooms I need? _____.

What is the minimum number of baths I need? _____.

If I don't have children today, am I willing to buy in an area with poor schools? _____.

Am I willing to purchase a home that requires repairs and painting if it means I'll do much of the work? _____.

Am I willing to purchase a home that requires repairs and painting if I *cannot* do much of the work? _____.

Am I willing to buy a home away from a particular religious institution or congregation? _____.

Am I willing to buy an apartment-style condo or a townhouse? _____.

If I have a choice between vacationing for a month or saving money for a home, which will I choose? _____.

variety of basic preferences. Having considered what you might like in a given property, we now come to the hard part: What trade-offs are you prepared to make?

The certain reality is that no home will possess every possible feature and benefit you prefer. *Even if money is not an issue, there is no perfect home.* Somehow, some way, there are always trade-offs to be made.

Would you exchange a longer commute for a lower price? This is the most common trade-off first-time buyers make.

Would you trade one less bedroom for a bigger kitchen or

living room? The issue here relates to utility. If you have an extra bedroom, what would you do with it? If you have more public space, more entertaining space, would that be more valuable within your circumstances and preferences?

In addition to commuting and space, we can also trade time and potential. Does it make sense to buy a small place today and save for a larger home tomorrow? If you save for the future and prices appreciate rapidly, will you be frozen out of the market?

If you are single now, will you buy a home large enough for two? Or three?

Trade-offs raise difficult issues. Simply stated, first-time buyers—like all buyers—will make trade-offs. The only remaining question is: What trade-offs are you prepared to make?

16

Contracts and Bargaining

Life as a consumer is filled with many benchmarks, and none is larger or more significant than the purchase of a home. In theory, at least, buying a house should be no more complicated than the acquisition of a car, refrigerator, or a bag of groceries. In reality, it doesn't work that way and for your protection, it shouldn't.

Imagine what would happen if all the usual protections, details, and checks were eliminated from the homebuying process. It seems simple and attractive, but as the Palmers are about to find out, real estate is like magic and quantum mechanics—nothing is quite as it seems.

It was a pleasant spring day when the Palmers decided to go house hunting. Married a year, they both worked and enjoyed an income and lifestyle that many people would envy. Driving along a country road, they found a three-bedroom Cape Cod with a large lot and a white picket fence, a perfect property for raising a family.

The Palmers stopped at the house and met with Mr. Barker, a genial fellow who introduced himself as the owner. He explained that the area within the fence amounted to nearly a full acre, that the house had just been fixed up, and that the property was available for $200,000.

The Palmers were not wealthy, but they told Barker that they had just inherited some money and wanted to make an offer. After some quibbling back and forth, the two sides quickly wrote out an agreement.

"In exchange for $190,000," the agreement said, "William Barker hereby agrees to sell his complete and total interests in a property known as 85 Maple Street to Ramona and Fritz Palmer, with closing to take place on the 25th of April. The undersigned buyers agree to accept the property in 'AS IS' condition and to pay a $5,000 deposit. The deposit shall be credited to the buyers at settlement."

Do we have a deal? In a perfect world we have an agreement between buyer and seller, we know the property's street address, the purchase price, the closing date, the deposit amount, and the fact that the deposit will be credited to the buyers at settlement. But the world is far from perfect, and the agreement between the Palmers and Barker is silent on several important matters.

There is no list of fixtures. *Fixtures* are items that convey to new owners when property is sold. Fixtures are usually defined as objects attached to a property and intended to remain with it, but fixtures can also be defined to include, or exclude, unattached items as well. In this case, there was a new washer and dryer the Palmers thought should come with the property, a thought seller Barker did not share.

No survey was required. Barker said the area within the fence was "nearly a full acre." "Nearly" is not a precise term, and when surveyed it turned out the property only had 35,000 square feet. An acre has 43,560 square feet and in this situation a full acre also has another value. In the community where Maple Street is located, homes with at least an acre of land can be subdivided into half-acre lots. The extra lot can then be sold off, effectively reducing the property's price.

A survey would also have shown that much of the new fence was actually located on a neighbor's lot, which means the neighbor may demand its removal.

There was no legal description of the property. As it turns out, the "property" surrounded by the white picket fence was actually located at 83 Maple Street, not 85 Maple Street.

No title search was required. Had the local land records been examined, the Palmers would have discovered that the property had once been used as a gasoline station. Considering this prior use, had the Palmers carefully checked the property they would have found that used motor oil had been dumped there. Whoever owns the Maple Street property might be responsible for cleaning an environmental hazard, a potentially expensive job.

No structural inspection was required.   If there's a problem with the house, if the basement leaks, the roof needs to be replaced, or the drains are clogged, the Palmers are stuck because they bought the property in "as is" condition.

The purchase did not depend on the availability of financing. Although the Palmers paid a $5,000 deposit, there is no provision for their money to be returned if they do not qualify for financing, or if financing at reasonable rates and terms is not available.

The agreement did not say who pays transfer taxes.   There's a 1 percent sales tax on real estate, in this case a $1,900 fee that someone must pay at closing.

The Palmers never bought a house!   What the Palmers purchased was not a particular house, but rather Barker's "complete and total" rights to a property at "85 Maple Street."

What rights does Barker hold? It's possible that Barker owns the property and has good title. It is also possible that he doesn't, that he bought the property from someone who was an alcoholic, insane, a drug user, or whose capacity to make a good contract is open to question. For all anyone knows, Barker has no ownership interest. If this sounds impossible, think about the individual who offered to sell an attractive townhouse at a very reasonable price, collected several offers and with them several large deposit checks, cashed the checks, and then migrated to a safe haven overseas. Who was this person? Someone who was housesitting and merely placed a for-sale ad in the local paper while the true owners were traveling.

OFFER AND ACCEPTANCE

The homebuying process is complex because there are many interests to protect. Buyers want their houses, sellers want their money, brokers want their commissions, lawyers want their fees, insurors want their premiums, governments want their taxes, and lenders want their security. Each and every interest is expressed or reflected in a single document, the sales contract.

A *sales contract* is nothing more than an agreement between buyers and sellers that transfers property ownership, at a specific price and terms, and on a particular date. It also includes *consideration,* something the purchaser puts up to assure the seller that the deal will be completed. A $5,000 deposit is one form of consideration.

To have a contract there must be an offer and there must be acceptance.

An *offer* is nothing more than a proposal, a suggestion that is not binding on anyone. If owner Hurst offers to sell his property for $180,000, buyers may accept or reject his offer.

If Hurst's offer is accepted, he will receive $180,000 for his property. If his offer is rejected, it's dead, finished, gone, over, and terminated unless he once again offers his property for sale at $180,000.

If a buyer hears that Hurst wants to sell his property for $180,000 and makes a $160,000 counter-offer, then Hurst's original offer is rejected. Now the $160,000 proposal is the offer under consideration.

Another buyer may respond differently. In this case the buyer may accept Hurst's $180,000 price but only if Hurst agrees to paint the living room. Since Hurst had offered his home for sale without a commitment to paint the living room, the purchaser has made a counter-offer.

A situation might also arise in which Hurst sees that his property is worth more than $180,000 and so decides to ask for more money. If a buyer comes along after Hurst withdraws his original offer, Hurst is not obligated to sell for $180,000 or any other price.

If Hurst and a buyer agree to a common set of terms and conditions, we then at least have the basis for a contract. But if the deal is sealed with only a handshake, problems can arise. With a verbal "deal," who knows what was said or unsaid? While Hurst and the buyer may believe they have an agreement, what happens if they misunderstand one another? Because verbal agreements are subject to dispute, only written contracts are generally enforceable in real estate.

Once there is a *written* contract between the parties, its terms and conditions can be modified only with the agreement of both buyer and seller, a key reason to assure that every detail and concern is properly addressed in the initial agreement.

AVOID BEGINNER'S LUCK

Sale agreements can be enormously complicated and the few words presented here are designed to provide only a brief and general introduction to the subject. It is because sale agreements are so complicated that first-time buyers should consult with a real estate attorney to work out proper language, to avoid pitfalls, and to assure that all rights are fully protected.

The fact that real estate agreements must be in writing offers many protections for both buyer and seller, assuming they're marketplace equals. But buyers and sellers are not equals—sellers have many advantages when dealing with purchasers and even more advantages when dealing with first-time buyers.

Residential sellers are typically represented by real estate brokers and agents, people familiar with realty agreements, who have marketplace experience, and who can materially assist property owners in the negotiating process.

Since the brokerage community typically represents seller interests, it should not come as a surprise that contract forms used by local brokers and agents—the nicely printed sheets that hold together so many real estate deals—commonly favor owners.

To understand how this occurs, consider a form where the buyer agrees to purchase a $110,000 property and finance the deal with a 10 percent mortgage or "the best available rate." Sounds perfectly safe and secure, but what happens if rates rise to 11 percent?

If $100,000 is being borrowed over 30 years, a 10 percent loan will have monthly payments of $877.57. If rates rise to 11 percent, monthly costs will go up to $952.32 and buyers will face a dilemma. Either they must accept the 11 percent interest figure since it is the "best available rate" or they can lose their deposit.

Lender guidelines may be the only protection available to buyers in a rising market. As rates rise, buyers become less and less qualified. If an agreement has a proper financing contingency, one that returns a buyer deposit if financing is unavailable, then steeply rising rates may allow buyers to withdraw from a deal without penalty. If rates do not rise steeply—if they rise enough to be uncomfortable but not so high that the buyer does not qualify for financing—then the purchaser is stuck.

A typical contract form protects the seller, because while the buyer can face significantly higher ownership costs, the seller is still collecting the full price for his property, even though higher interest rates suggest less demand and lower prices.

One could argue that if interest rates fall, the seller's property might be worth more. True, but the seller need not worry about whether rates rise or fall; his deal is known and in hand. It's the buyer who faces uncertainty and risk.

No one says contract forms have to be "fair" or "balanced," and typically they aren't. As a first-time buyer it makes sense to accept the reality that the form you use to purchase real estate will probably be provided by a broker or agent working for the seller and that it will favor the property owner.

It also makes sense to protect your interests. No matter what anyone tells you, contract forms can be modified, changed, or enhanced to customize your deal. There may be widely used forms, there may be forms that most people accept without change, there may be forms described as the "standard form we always use," but for you, the first-time buyer, accepting such forms at face value can be a disaster.

At some point we are all beginners. There are college freshmen, baseball rookies, and first-time offenders, and if there's a single quality that ties beginners together, it's a lack of experience which leads to mistakes.

The trouble is that real estate is a big-ticket item. Make a mistake and it can be expensive. Very expensive. So expensive that you may need years to pay for a single error.

For first-time buyers, there is a plain and simple approach that can save grief, anguish, and cash. *Hire someone with experience, someone who knows about real estate and can help you with the bargaining process.* After all, if professional help is a good idea for sellers, why not buyers?

GETTING HELP

There are several people who can do much to enhance your marketplace position as a first-time buyer. To get the most value from real estate professionals, be sure you hire them *before* the house hunting process begins. It is important to line up a supporting cast of experts at the earliest possible time because the alternative—trying to locate professional help after you find a home—means you will be pressed for time and perhaps unable to locate the best possible assistance.

You need a local lawyer, someone who deals extensively in real estate and can act as your advocate. An attorney should be able to review contract forms with you, explain the meaning and implication of various clauses, and suggest suitable modifications and changes.

Although sellers and brokers often dislike the use of attorneys, you have your interests to protect. Your lawyer is obligated to serve you with total fidelity and to employ his or her professional training and experience for your benefit alone.

To find an attorney, get recommendations from recent buyers. Also speak with lawyers who offer settlement services. Ask several attorneys about their rates, experience with other buyers, and willingness to work with you.

You will also need a structural inspector, preferably a member of the American Society of Home Inspectors (ASHI). (Look under "Inspection Bureaus" or "Building Inspection Services" in the phone book.)

A structural inspection allows you to have a knowledgeable individual go through a house and check every component, look for leaks, breaks, and decay, and pinpoint repairs that may be required now or in the near future. If you use a structural inspector, do not be surprised if a pristine house that looks wonderful actually contains a lengthy list of minor problems. Houses are complex and none is perfect.

When a purchase depends on a "satisfactory" inspection, then problems that are costly or that threaten health and safety may cause buyers to reconsider the deal. Perhaps the property can only be regarded as satisfactory if the price is lower so that more funds will be available for repairs. Perhaps the deal will be workable only if sellers make repairs by closing. Or, perhaps, the best choice is simply to terminate the transaction and have the deposit returned.

Another professional who can help is the same one upon whom sellers rely, the broker. Although brokers typically serve sellers, real estate laws commonly state that brokers and their agents are licensed to assist those who sell, purchase, exchange, lease, or manage real estate. In effect, brokers can represent either sellers or buyers, though not both at the same time without express written permission from each party in advance.

17

Buyer Representation

Because little in real estate is simple or straightforward, it should come as little surprise that the marketing system itself—the way in which homes are represented, advertised, priced, and sold—is far more complicated than first appearances might suggest.

To start, we have brokers and agents. *Brokers* are licensed individuals who can assist others, for a fee, in the purchase, sale, exchange, rental, or management of real estate. *Agents* are licensed, but they can only work under the direction of a real estate broker.

In the eyes of the brokerage community, the world is divided into clients and customers. Clients pay brokers for their professional services. In turn, brokers have an *agency relationship* with clients, an obligation to represent clients and to get the best possible price and terms for them.

Customers are not clients. They're individuals with whom brokers interact, but since they do not pay for brokerage services, customers are not entitled to the benefits of brokerage representation.

In most real estate transactions, brokers and agents work for sellers, represent sellers, and—because they represent sellers—their job is to obtain the best possible price and terms for property owners.

As for buyers, they are customers. Brokers typically do not work for buyers, are not paid by buyers, and have no obligation to find the best possible price and terms for buyers.

Unfortunately, many buyers do not understand how real estate is marketed or the broker's role. A Federal Trade Commission staff report has shown that 74.2 percent of all home buyers thought their interests were represented by real estate brokers and agents. Because of such misunderstandings, purchasers commonly rely on brokers and agents for market information, pricing, and the contract forms used to create deals.

It's enormously important for first-time buyers to understand the broker's role and to use the services brokers and agents can provide in their position as seller representatives. A selected list of such services shows that brokers and agents can:

- Introduce buyers to properties in a given area or price range.
- State prices at which individual properties are listed.
- Describe features that make individual properties unique and interesting.
- Tell what an individual seller is offering with the house, if anything. For example, a broker can state if a clothes washer and dryer are included in the list price, or if an outdoor play set conveys.
- List school districts that serve individual properties.
- List past sales and current listings for a given area.
- Suggest financing sources and current rates and terms.
- Provide information such as yearly property taxes, lot sizes, and utility information.
- Supply items such as surveys, lease agreements, floor plans, etc. *Note that when property is leased, new owners are bound by rental agreements.*

The list above contains significant omissions. It does not say, for example, that a seller's broker can represent you, negotiate on your behalf, or suggest a lower sale price.

LISTINGS AND MLS SYSTEMS

One broker working for one seller is easy to comprehend. Matters become more complex when a broker drives you to nine separate homes in a single afternoon. Since each house is presumably owned by a different individual, does the broker then work for each owner? Yes. Here's how.

To understand how this happens, first-time buyers need to know about sub-agency and a related topic, fee-splitting.

To represent a seller, a broker must have an employment contract known as a listing agreement. A *listing agreement* gives brokers the right to market a property at a particular price and under certain conditions for a given period, say 60 to 90 days. (Note that while a real estate *agent* may physically list the property, the actual agreement is between the seller and a *broker*. Agents work for brokers and have no right to list property directly.)

In addition to price, a listing agreement may also show how many points a seller is willing to pay and the deposit amount required to create an acceptable offer.

To market a residential property, sellers typically agree to proportional fees—say 6 percent of the entire sale price. Because commissions are proportional, they rise in value as property prices increase and decrease in value when sale prices decline.

Once a property is listed, the broker then tries to sell it. He not only advertises the property and holds open houses, but he also cooperates with other brokers, either informally or through a local *multiple listing system,* or MLS.

An MLS can be seen from three perspectives. In one sense, it's an advertising medium that lists currently available properties.

An MLS also resembles a research library. A member can look up properties by address, neighborhood, and price, or by such features as the number of bedrooms, baths, or zoning. Past prices and current listings can be checked.

In addition to roles as an advertising medium and reference, most MLS systems also enable members to represent individual sellers through a process called *sub-agency.*

The broker who lists a property is the seller's agent. Other MLS members are not agents because they did not list the property. Instead, other brokers are sub-agents who have the right to show the property *through* the original listing agreement. It is through sub-agency that brokers can take purchasers to various homes and represent each owner.

The broker who lists the property is known as the *listing broker* and the broker who locates a purchaser is called the *selling broker*. If a property is sold for $125,000 with a 6 percent fee, the commission might be divided along the following lines:

- If the listing broker sells the property, he or she receives the entire commission, $7,500.

- If an agent working for the listing broker lists or sells the property, the broker and agent split the commission according to whatever arrangement they have, perhaps 50/50. Now the broker is paid $7,500 by the seller and the broker, in turn, pays the agent $3,750.

- If the property is listed by one broker and a buyer is located by a second broker, the fee is divided between the brokers. Each broker receives $3,750.

- If an agent working for one broker lists the property, and an agent working for another broker sells the property, the $7,500 fee is divided between the two brokers. Each broker receives $3,750 and then divides the commission with his or her agent. If the agents split 50/50 with their brokers, then each agent receives $1,875. (See Table 33.)

Commissions are earned when the precise terms of the listing agreement have been met. If an offer to purchase is made for less than the full asking price, or if one or more listing terms are changed, then the listing agreement has not been fully satisfied and it is possible for a seller to reject a deal and not owe a brokerage commission. Conversely, if the offer meets the listing's terms and conditions, then the broker has earned his or her fee.

Brokers can work for sellers. Brokers can work for buyers. Can brokers work for both buyers and sellers at the same time? In rare situations, such as a property exchange where both parties have supplied written approval in advance, yes. In a residential sale transaction such arrangements are unusual.

To clarify the broker's role, many real estate groups are pressing for mandatory, written disclosures by brokers and agents up front so there is no question about the broker's obligations and loyalties. Many states now require such disclosures and it is

Table 33 BROKERAGE FLOW CHART

Sale Price	$125,000
Commission	6 percent
Commission Value	$7,500
Broker A Lists and Sells	$7,500
Broker A Lists, Broker B Sells, Each Receives	$3,750
Broker A Lists, Agent A Sells, Each Receives	$3,750
Broker A Lists, Agent B Sells, Broker A and Broker B Receive	$3,750
Broker B and Agent B Split $3,750, Each Receives	$1,875
Agent A Lists, Agent B Sells, Broker A and Broker B Receive	$3,750
Broker A Splits with Agent A	$1,875
Broker B Splits with Agent B	$1,875

hoped the next time the Federal Trade Commission surveys the real estate market, more buyers will understand how it works.

Not only is disclosure becoming more common, but another trend is also beginning to emerge. More and more frequently, buyers are hiring brokers to represent them.

BUYER BROKERS

Brokers who work for purchasers are described as *buyer brokers* and they can offer important services. While an attorney understands contracts and legal language, a good broker knows the marketplace, values, and negotiation strategies.

To understand how buyer brokers work, consider first how seller representation is used. Owners who hire brokers have the advantage of the broker's skills, experience, and training, plus access to the agency/sub-agency system. In exchange, sellers typically pay a proportional fee, say 6 to 7 percent of the entire sale price. Since commission values rise along with sale prices, brokers have a clear incentive to favor the highest possible prices for a given property.

A buyer broker can receive a fee for locating a property that meets the purchaser's precise needs, for acting as a consultant to a purchaser, or both.

As a *finder,* a broker can identify possible properties, help the buyer evaluate housing options, and then assist in the negotiation process. Unlike the seller's representative, a buyer broker is not obligated to an owner and can suggest sale prices and terms that differ markedly from listing agreements.

As a *consultant* a buyer broker can assist in negotiations, examine comparable housing prices, and devise purchasing strategies.

Unlike a seller representative who is usually paid a proportional fee based on the final sale price, a buyer broker can be paid with a fixed fee established up front. A purchaser can "list" his or her needs with a broker and if the broker finds an acceptable property within a given time frame and negotiates a successful transaction, then the fee established in advance will be due and payable at closing.

Buyer brokers can also be paid with hourly fees, the form of payment used most commonly by those who act as consultants.

It is also possible to retain buyer brokers with mixed fees. For instance, a broker can receive a finder's fee as well as an hourly fee. Buyer and broker might agree that the broker will be compensated for a minimum number of hours so that if no acceptable house is found, the broker receives compensation for his or her time and effort. If a property is found, any hourly charges paid to the broker are deducted from the finder's fee. This type of payment strategy assures some compensation to the broker without allowing excessive costs if a property is found.

HOW TO FIND A BUYER BROKER

While buyer brokerage is becoming more common, and while all brokers are licensed to represent purchasers, most brokers and their agents continue to represent sellers, if only as a matter of custom. For these reasons, finding a buyer broker may not be easy.

One resource that may help is the most recent edition of *The*

Buyer's Brokerage Registry ($27.50 including postage and handling, P.O. Box 23275, Ventura, CA 93002; 805–643–2337). This guide's attraction is that only *experienced* buyer brokers are listed.

Other sources include:

- Professional real estate groups in your community.
- Attorneys with active real estate practices.
- Purchasers who have used buyer brokers.
- Brokers who advertise buyer representation services.
- Instructors who offer buyer brokerage classes at colleges and universities.

BUYER BROKERAGE AGREEMENTS

Once a buyer representative is found, it pays to sit down and discuss your needs in detail and determine what services the broker can offer. If the services have value, if the broker has experience, and if the broker can materially improve your ability to get a good deal, then it may make sense to hire a buyer broker.

If you hire a broker with an hourly agreement, care should be taken to assure that you are billed for "approved" hours only. Also, the matter of *which* hours are billable should be clarified. For example, if a broker spends one hour in conference with you, or one hour with a seller, that clearly is billable time. But what about time traveling to a property and back? What about time spent with an MLS computer? How should the broker account for such time and effort?

As to an hourly rate, to see what's reasonable consider the fees area professionals earn in such fields as law, accounting, or engineering. See what the broker proposes.

When hiring a buyer representative, be certain the employment agreement reflects your interests and requirements. It should show both your obligations and those of the broker as well as the type of property being sought, a specific price range, an acceptable location, the agreement's length (say 60 or 90 days), and any special features you require.

CONFLICTS

While buyer brokerage has attractions, it is not now a common practice and purchasers should be alert to several potential conflicts.

First, what happens if a buyer wants to purchase a home *listed* by the broker? In this situation a broker might receive compensation from each party, but only with their prior knowledge and approval. A better approach is to have the broker stop representing one party or the other. As a practical matter, it's the buyer brokerage relationship that should be terminated.

If a brokerage arrangement ends because a purchaser wants to buy a home listed by a broker, then any offer to the property owner should contain a statement detailing the past relationship between the broker and purchaser. This not only is fair to the owner, but also prevents future claims by an owner who might otherwise claim that the relationship between the purchaser and broker was hidden.

Also, if a purchaser wants to buy property listed by a buyer broker, then any fees paid previously by the purchaser should be returned at closing.

A more complex conflict is possible when one agent acts as a buyer broker, a second agent represents a seller, and both agents work for the same broker. Even though the agents represent different parties, one broker is collecting fees from both sides of the table. Since agents can only work through the authority of a broker, it is, in fact, the broker who must represent both sides. In such situations, it can make sense for the buyer's agent to withdraw and for the two agents to work out compensation within the brokerage firm.

Second, an agreement ought to say that a real estate broker can offer ideas, advice, and information within his or her sphere of knowledge and that buyers should seek advice from appropriate professionals as necessary, such as attorneys, accountants, engineers, or architects.

Third, so that sellers and their brokers are not confused or perplexed, buyer brokers should always state who they represent, purchasers should tell sellers and their representatives if they are using a buyer broker, and all offers should plainly describe any relationship between a buyer and a buyer's broker.

18

Buyer Brokerage
and Lender Policies

We have just seen how buyer brokerage can help first-time buyers gain marketplace equality. Given the advantages of such assistance, one might think that lenders would be eager to encourage buyer brokerage, since a good deal for purchasers translates into more security for lenders.

If there is one trait which marks the mortgage borrowing process, it's unrelenting caution. Try to get a loan and lenders automatically seek credit checks, surveys, title searches, title insurance, private mortgage insurance, and a variety of reserves and prepayments. Yet such protections are established only after the deal is finished, after buyer and seller have agreed to a particular price and terms.

Thus we have a system where, if a purchaser does not make the best possible deal, it's not an issue as long as the lender's interests are protected. In effect, there is no weaker link in the homebuying process than the average buyer, especially one purchasing for the first time.

Nowhere in the lending system is there an effort to take the most obvious precaution of all, to have someone represent the purchaser *before* he or she enters into a deal. Surely lenders would be better off if purchasers did not pay maximum prices or various closing expenses as a matter of custom, tradition, or fine print.

Given these advantages, one might expect that lenders would be elated with buyer representation, but that's not the case. If a house sells for $150,000 and the owner pays a 6 percent broker-age fee, lenders don't care. But if the same house sells for $146,000, the seller pays a $4,000 fee, and the buyer pays a separate $4,000 fee, most lenders will finance the property on the basis of its $146,000 acquisition cost. Thus we have a system where the seller's marketplace representation is underwritten, but the buyer's is not.

Lender standards do not deny purchasers the right to hire buyer brokers. All lenders say, typically, is that if buyers want broker representation, such services cannot be funded with mortgage financing. In practical terms, most buyers can hardly afford toothpaste at the time they purchase a home, much less brokerage fees, and the result of lender policies is not only to deny, restrict, and limit buyer options in the marketplace, but to assure that purchasers rely on sellers and their agents, folks who in good faith have a perfect right to seek the highest possible property prices.

Consider the positions taken by two of the most significant, and most pro-borrower, players in the mortgage game, the Federal Housing Administration and the Veterans Administration.

Under FHA rules a finder's fee to a broker may be allowed if the loan does not exceed the appraised cost—that is, the sale price plus allowable closing expenses. If a home sells for $90,000, closing costs are $1,000, and the purchaser wants to finance a $2,700 buyer brokerage fee, that's okay with FHA, providing the property is worth more than the sale price. In this example, the property must appraise at $93,700 to cover acquisition, closing, and buyer brokerage expenses.

There is an important exception to general FHA regulations. If a local FHA field office feels that a brokerage fee for the purpose of finding a property is a customary charge, it can be included among acceptable closing costs.

The VA, says department loan specialist Gerald Ferrence, has had a "consistent interpretation that brokerage fees are prohibited." The VA's position is based on two points. First, the payment of brokerage fees is not expressly allowed. Second, under CFR 3643.12 (c), it says that "brokerage or other charges shall not be made against the veteran for obtaining any guarantee or insurance," a provision that has been interpreted to include real estate brokerage fees.

To avoid problems with lender policies, some buyer brokers have adopted payment plans that work like this: In the case of a $150,000 sale with a 6 percent commission, the selling broker receives $9,000. As part of the deal, the selling broker is then required to assign a portion of the commission to the buyer broker.

This approach is neither neat nor tidy. It is entirely possible that the selling broker is not getting a 6 percent commission, in which case the buyer's broker may be working for small change. More importantly, the relationship between the buyer broker and the purchaser is diluted, in appearance if not in fact, by payments through the seller's representative.

Also, it should be said that assigning brokerage fees may also raise a contractual issue. Unlike buyers and sellers, brokers are not principals in a real estate transaction. The listing broker's relationship with a seller is a separate matter established with a separate contract, the listing agreement. *With a full-price offer that meets all the terms and conditions of a listing agreement,* one has to wonder if sellers, buyers, and buyer brokers have any right to propose terms that may effectively represent a revision of the listing broker's original commission arrangement.

Another strategy works like this: Rather than pay any portion of a purchaser's buyer brokerage commission, a seller merely gives a credit to the buyer at closing. A seller, for example, might credit a purchaser with $4,500 to offset closing costs. Whether this money is used to pay transfer taxes, points, or brokerage fees, it still lowers buyer acquisition expenses.

This strategy is less than perfect. Sellers are not thrilled by the thought of giving credits, and lenders routinely limit seller contributions so they are not disproportionate to the deal. Also, seller contributions may not even be allowed unless the contract agreement specifically states why a credit is being given. With the VA, for instance, seller credits are permitted for certain purposes, but not others. Money from a seller to pay a buyer's personal debts is not acceptable under VA rules.

While lender guidelines were established many years ago, the marketplace has changed. There are now more than 30 states that require brokers to disclose for whom they work, disclosures that raise an obvious point: If brokers can work for sellers, they can also work for buyers. Mandatory disclosure, as much as any

other factor, has made buyer representation increasingly common.

Lenders have always sought to protect their interests, and no
one begrudges their right to do so. Many guidelines now in place
were designed to shield purchasers from excess fees and unnecessary charges. But has not the time come to amend aged
rules and concepts, to recognize that both lenders and borrowers
share the benefits of a good deal and the risks of a bad one, and
to understand that without representation buyers cannot compete as marketplace equals with sellers? Most importantly, is it
not true that those purchasers least able to defend themselves—
first-time buyers and those who are not financially sophis-
ticated—suffer most from current lender policies?

Lender guidelines change constantly and there is no reason
why new rules encouraging buyer representation should be
avoided. If fees for buyer brokerage payments can be readily
funded with mortgage financing, several trends will unfold.

First, no less than a survey or title search, buyer brokerage
ultimately assures that purchasers are getting a good deal and
thus lender risk is reduced. Surely some portion of the enormous
losses now faced by lenders might have been avoided if purchasers made buying decisions with the aid of experienced, trained
realty professionals.

Second, buyer brokerage will grow if such services can be
funded over many years.

Third, those buyer brokers who now look to listing brokers for
compensation assignments will no longer have any reason to do
so. With updated lender policies, they can be paid directly by
purchasers and avoid any hint of conflict.

Fourth, as buyer brokerage becomes more common, listing
agreements and standardized sales contracts will each address
the issue of payments to buyer representatives—that is, how
listing brokers are to be paid in the event that a buyer broker
participates in a transaction. Including provisions for buyer brokerage in both listing and sale agreements will resolve many
issues in advance.

From a lending perspective, a shift in guidelines should assure
both that buyer brokerage is a viable option for purchasers and
that total brokerage fees do not expand to disproportionate or
unconscionable levels. Deals where listing brokers are required

to assign a portion of their commission to buyer representatives should be prohibited, if only because they diminish the appearance of separate representation.

The issues raised here will not disappear. Each time a state enacts a mandatory disclosure rule, each time a would-be purchaser signs a disclosure form, the representation issue is raised. As the number of transactions involving buyer brokers increases, the concept will become more familiar to the public and more widely accepted within the brokerage community. Mortgage guidelines that now discourage buyer brokerage should be revised, if only as a matter of lender self-interest.

FOR SALE BY OWNER

We have looked at the use of brokers in the marketing system, but not all homes are sold through the brokerage community. A small proportion are marketed directly by owners, often in an effort to save the brokerage fee.

There is nothing wrong with buying a home marketed by an owner, but buyers who do so should recognize that the lack of a broker in the transaction may mean more work for both buyer and seller.

When a home is sold as a *for sale by owner*, or "Fizzbo," there's no broker to provide offer forms, suggest financing, or negotiate a deal. Since brokers typically represent sellers, Fizzbos effectively give up some of the marketplace advantages available to other sellers.

The lack of broker representation may present attractive opportunities to first-time purchasers. You can supply your own offer forms and suggest attractive financing. Buyers who use an attorney or a buyer broker, or both, are also likely to have a significant negotiating advantage.

As for the brokerage commission that is not being paid, there is no rule which says it should go entirely to the seller in the form of a full sale price. If the owner has had problems selling the property, perhaps a discount in price equal to half the commission would be appropriate. If the seller has had severe marketing problems, perhaps an amount equal to the entire commission could be used to offset the sale price. At the very least, the value of the brokerage commission should be seen as a negotiable item.

19

Contracts

No matter where a home is located or how much it costs, at some point every aspect of a real estate deal must be committed to writing. The document that holds the deal together must be carefully written to prevent misunderstandings, conflicts, and legal entanglements. Contracts not only must outline the complete transaction, they also must anticipate potential disputes and resolve them before problems arise.

As a purchaser it's probable that you will encounter offer forms used by local real estate brokers. Get a copy from a broker or attorney, study it with care, and then have a broker, attorney, or both explain what each item means and how problem areas should be handled. Watch out for short contract forms (important issues are often omitted) or forms available for use nation-wide (local areas may have specific transaction requirements such as notices that must be spelled out in an agreement).

As a purchaser you can modify a form, strike out language you don't like, and add conditions important to you. *A printed form is not sacred, so don't be afraid to change it.*

Most areas have several local forms, so find the one that treats you best and use it to make your offer. If you use a pro-seller form that requires numerous modifications, if items are scratched out, penciled in and added on, then a seller will surely notice your handiwork and the provisions you want will be open to debate. It's easier to win concessions if they are perceived as routine, provisions in the body of the contract that just happen to be part of the deal.

While you have a right to modify and change agreements, as a matter of self-interest you also have an obligation to do it correctly. Unless you are trained as a broker or agent, you will need professional help to amend form agreements.

Help can come from real estate professionals, brokers and agents who write offers and modify contract forms. In some jurisdictions, however, only lawyers can develop or modify *written* agreements. Because of occupational limitations, in some states it can happen that although brokers hold the key to successful negotiating strategies, attorneys are required to convert such strategies into acceptable contract language.

What are the issues first-time buyers should consider? Here is a *selected* list of important topics that every offer form should address:

Address.   Where is the property? You'll need both a street address (12 Main Street) and a legal description, a form of address that typically includes such items as the lot, block, and square recorded in local government records (Lot 8, Block 9, Square 14 of the subdivision known as Fortune Acres). The legal address shows that both buyer and seller are talking about the same property.

Agency.   Brokers participate in the overwhelming majority of all residential sales, so it's not surprising that standardized forms leave space to name the broker or brokers who put the deal together.

There was a time when offer forms listed the broker's commission, but in many areas this practice has disappeared, and with good reason.

Unlike buyers and sellers, brokers are not principals in a real estate transaction. The broker typically works for the seller and the broker's commission is established in a separate agreement, the listing contract.

The broker's fee is a matter for the seller and broker to work out. If your offer is less than the seller anticipated, then as a condition of accepting the offer the owner may want to renegotiate the broker's fee. If so, it's a matter between the broker and the seller.

Another reason commissions are rarely shown today has to do with anti-trust issues. If brokers must show their commissions, then other brokers will know how much is being charged, information that invites peer pressure and conformity.

Assignment. As a purchaser you want the right to assign the agreement. It can happen that others want the property and with a right to assign you can sell your interest. In this instance, your "interest" is not the property, but rather the *right* to buy it at given rates and terms.

Assumptions. Forms often require purchasers to pay all loan assumption fees. In reality, this is a negotiable item, as is everything else.

Closing. This is the date when settlement is required, usually with the proviso that settlement can be delayed if there are problems with the title or survey. Buyers should expect closing in 45 to 60 days in most cases, sometimes less if loan documents can be processed quickly. Interestingly, the general practice is that east of the Mississippi buyers select settlement providers. West of the Mississippi, sellers decide who will conduct closing.

Condition. A property is supposed to be left "broom clean" by sellers, an expression that says nothing about bathtub rings or oven grime.

More importantly from the buyer's perspective, the property should be free and clear of all debris, especially items that may require hauling. Mattresses and old appliances are particularly difficult to unload in many areas because regular trash removal services will not take them. If the contract requires a broom clean property and large items have been left behind, then money from the seller should be set aside to assure their removal.

Credit Release. Buried in many form agreements is permission for lenders to examine credit reports and for brokers to release financial information given to them by purchasers.

Damages.   Deposits and damages are closely related. Fail to complete the deal without good cause and you may be liable for damages.

Damages can be assessed in the form of a lost deposit, money damages, and in rare cases a requirement to go through with the deal. As a purchaser you want to offer a small deposit. You also want to assure that you cannot be liable for any damages other than the deposit.

Deposits.   A contract requires offer and acceptance, and it typically demands "consideration" as well, evidence that the purchaser will go through with the deal. A deposit is one form of consideration, money put up by the purchaser at the time an offer is accepted.

Deposits raise several issues that first-time buyers should regard with care.

First, how much should you put down? There is no "standard" deposit and as a purchaser you should put down as little as possible. For a $100,000 purchase, anything from $1,000 to $10,000 might be acceptable, though buyers should certainly prefer the lower figure.

Second, who will hold the deposit? When a home is sold by a real estate broker, the deposit is usually placed in the broker's escrow account, an account that is separate and apart from the broker's funds. *When offering a deposit, endorse the check so that it can only be deposited in an escrow account.*

If a property is being marketed by a self-seller, the issue of holding deposits becomes sticky. From your perspective as a purchaser, it may pay to suggest establishing an escrow account that requires both your signature and the seller's before any funds can be withdrawn.

Third, if the deposit is in escrow, is interest paid on the account? Buyers should demand that their money is placed in an interest-bearing account and that any interest is credited to them at closing.

Fourth, under what conditions can the deposit be lost? If you back out of the deal, then clearly the deposit should go to the seller. But what if you can't get financing at the rates and terms cited in the contract? What if the deal falls through because the seller will not make required repairs? A well-written offer can resolve such issues in your favor.

Financing.   A contract form will spell out financing terms with some precision, though usually not enough for buyers.

A form might say that you will make a 5 percent down payment and then show the amount to be borrowed; whether the loan has a fixed or adjustable rate; and whether the financing will be conventional, VA, or FHA. Note that deposits and down payments are likely to be different amounts.

The problem for first-time buyers is that forms often contain language that contradicts quoted rates and terms. A nicely printed form may have appropriate blanks for the loan amount, interest rate, and monthly payment. The same form may also say that if the exact loan terms are not available, then the purchaser must accept the "best rate prevailing at the time of closing." Such language means that if the buyer agrees to 10 percent financing but the "best" available rate is 11 percent, the purchaser must accept the higher interest rate or possibly lose his or her deposit.

Buyers will want to spell out acceptable rates and terms and eliminate language that creates open-ended financial obligations.

Fixtures.   We usually define property as land and the improvements on the land, items such as houses or garages. In addition, other items typically become the buyer's when property is sold, items attached to the property and intended to be part of it, items called *fixtures*.

A furnace is certainly a fixture. It's attached to the property, intended to be part of the property, and not something that one can casually move. In contrast, a counter-top microwave oven can be unplugged and removed at any time.

Many contract forms list items that are regarded as fixtures, such as window shades, carpets, trees, shrubs, shutters, and awnings. The important point is that through the magic of good contract language, fixtures can be created. You want the washer and dryer? If your offer says the clothes washer and dryer go to the purchaser at settlement, they're yours if the seller accepts the offer.

Insurance. In addition to title insurance, there are two additional forms of coverage that are important in property transactions.

First, to get a mortgage, lenders will insist that you have adequate fire, theft, and liability insurance. Ask the lender how much insurance is regarded as adequate and when the paid-in-full policy needs to be delivered—either a few days before closing or at the settlement table.

Second, you need to examine the contract form carefully to see who is responsible for maintaining property insurance once the property is under contract but title has not been transferred. Practices around the country vary, but buyers can insist that sellers remain liable until title has been conveyed and that their liability insurance continues in force until *recordation.* Note that recordation—transferring title in local records—usually takes place several days after closing.

Lender Requirements. Some forms obligate sellers to abide by "reasonable" lender repair requirements. This is one of the few instances where form agreements create an open-ended requirement for sellers. Who knows what "reasonable" repairs might include or how much they might cost?

Lender requirements are also presented indirectly. For instance, a requirement to promptly apply for financing will require purchasers to find a lender. But lenders will only make loans with their forms, forms that conveniently require buyer/borrowers to pay a variety of costs and fees, to have required insurance, to obtain a survey, to have insurance, to provide credit information, etc.

Ownership. As a purchaser you can buy property by yourself as a *sole proprietor,* or you can buy with others.

Different ownership arrangements reflect different rights. Married couples typically buy property as a *tenancy by the entireties.* With this type of ownership, each spouse has a complete interest in the property, something that is important in the face of bankruptcies, estate taxes, divorces, and other matters.

In some states, married partners may own real estate under community property rules. The basic idea with community property is that any real estate acquired during marriage belongs equally to both parties.

Those not married may elect to buy together in a *joint tenancy*. If one party dies *and* there is an automatic right of survivorship, then property interests can pass directly to other owners. To have a joint tenancy each party must have an equal ownership interest, in addition to other requirements.

A *tenancy in common* represents ownership between two or more people where interests need not be identical, where interests can be sold or willed individually, and where survivorship is not automatic.

Ownership matters can be complex and should not be considered without legal advice. Also, ownership issues should encourage each prospective buyer to create a will, another subject to discuss with a lawyer.

Points. Not only can interest rates rise and fall between the time a contract is signed and closing, but the number of points associated with a loan can also vary over time. Contract forms may outline a basic obligation to pay points, say 1 point at closing from the buyer and 1 point from the seller.

Such forms may then say that the purchaser shall accept any "reasonable" lender requirement for points and loan origination fees at settlement, even if the requirement is different from the number of points stated in the contract.

When such language is used buyers can be hurt in two ways. First, the form creates an open-ended commitment to pay whatever points a lender elects to charge, a potentially serious matter when rates and points have not been locked in. Second, while printed forms often create an open-ended commitment for buyers, sellers are routinely spared such obligations.

Buyers should be certain that offer forms limit the requirement to pay points and that open-ended language is eliminated. If possible, have the seller pay all points, loan discount fees, and origination charges, something that may be possible in a weak market.

Possession. Most agreements clearly show that once settlement takes place the property belongs to the purchaser, and the seller and the seller's goods are to be off the property.

Price.   What is the property's complete and total sale price? The price is usually written out both numerically ($108,500) and in words (one hundred and eight thousand five hundred dollars and no cents).

As a first-time buyer you want to offer enough so that your deal is plausible, but not so much that you overpay. In thinking about prices, consider recent sales of like properties in the same area, the property's condition, the length of time the home has been on the market, and the reason the property is for sale.

Sellers market their properties for different reasons and it's perfectly proper to ask why a home is being sold. Those with financial problems, tax difficulties, or a need to move are often more flexible than other sellers, *flexible* meaning they will take a lower price or accept terms more favorable to the buyer.

Estate sales can be attractive if there is a need to promptly pay inheritance taxes. Those getting divorced are often elated to unload their homes, even at reduced prices.

Individuals who have missed mortgage payments and face foreclosure will often sell at discount, but only if they can get a reasonable price and preserve some of their equity. Sale notices can be found in local newspapers, but buyers contacting distressed sellers should be careful. In some areas making a low-ball offer to a homeseller who faces foreclosure may be regarded as "unconscionable" and grounds for legal action against would-be buyers.

Qualification Letter.   More and more sellers are requiring buyers to quickly apply for financing and to obtain a lender letter stating that they, the purchasers, appear likely to qualify for the required loan.

Like chess, each real estate move creates a counter-move and to satisfy such requirements, lenders routinely issue qualification letters, or as many call them, *hand-holding letters.* Such letters typically state that on the basis of the purchaser's income, it appears likely that the buyer will qualify for financing, subject to verification of the purchaser's income and debts, as well as a satisfactory appraisal and survey of the property. Such caveats assure that lenders have no obligation to actually make a loan.

Renting.   An offer form should prohibit sellers from renting the property once a contract has been ratified. Renting obligates the buyer to any lease terms established between seller and tenant and denies occupancy to the purchaser.

Another potential problem concerns rent control. Two hundred communities have rent control rules, and it's possible that even a temporary lease agreement can give tenants a right to buy the property as well as other benefits.

Termite Inspection.   Buyers will be required to hire a pest inspector at their expense and provide the lender with evidence that the property is free and clear of termites and other wood-boring insects. Depending how the form agreement is worded, if infestation is found the owner is typically required to exterminate any pest infestations and repair structural damage.

Title.   When property is purchased there is an assumption that the seller is in fact the owner, has good title, and that the title can convey to the purchaser without problems. Such assumptions are sometimes wrong.

All property sales should be contingent on a title examination conducted by the purchaser's attorney or title company showing that the seller owns the property, has clear title, and that all unwanted liens and claims have been eliminated by closing. Note that in some situations you will want to leave liens and claims intact. For example, you don't want the seller to pay off a loan you intend to assume.

Deals where purchasers are offered a quit-claim deed should be avoided unless the transaction is first reviewed by *your* attorney. A *quit-claim deed* says merely that the seller transfers whatever interest he or she has in the property.

If title is faulty, or if the seller refuses to remedy title defects or to remove various liens and claims, then purchasers should have the right to back out of the deal without penalty. In addition, deposits should be refunded in full and purchasers should be reimbursed for any expenses associated with the title search.

A *title search* is designed to trace the property's ownership through local government records as far back as possible, sometimes into colonial times. A *title abstract* is a summary of the information found in local records.

A search of local records, however, should not be enough to satisfy first-time buyers. It is possible that such records may be incomplete or in error. Worse, they may not reveal substantial problems. For example, if a former owner was a drunk, someone lacking the legal capacity to convey title, or someone whose capacity may be in question, then title claims can arise even though the local records seem clean and pure.

To protect yourself, insist on *title insurance*, policies that protect you if a title dispute or problem arises. Title insurance is typically available in two forms: *Lender's coverage* will protect you up to the outstanding value of the mortgage—as the mortgage balance goes down, so does coverage. *Owner's coverage* will protect you up to the property's purchase price, coverage that means your down payment is insured against title problems.

Lenders will insist on coverage up to the loan's outstanding value; thus lender's coverage is not an option for most purchasers. Owner's coverage is optional, but recommended. Why is title insurance recommended? Personal experience.

One day the sheriff knocked on the door and handed me a subpoena. It seemed that some property I owned was at the center of a dispute between the former owner and a would-be purchaser. If the purchaser's claims were accepted, then perhaps title to "my" property would be in question. It was at this moment that title insurance seemed wonderfully comforting, especially since such policies not only protect against claims, but also underwrite legal costs.

While title insurance as a product may be comforting, the marketing practices that accompany such policies should be monitored with care.

- Title insurance may be available with various endorsements. For example, an inflation rider will raise owner's coverage as the property's value increases. Other endorsements may limit coverage if, for example, a survey was inaccurate.

- Be aware that in some jurisdictions attorneys receive significant fees by selling title insurance. Sale commissions that exceed 50 percent of the entire premium have been documented.

- Title insurance costs can be reduced in many cases when policies are re-issued. Re-issue rates that save buyers 10 to 20
percent are often available when properties are being re-sold
after a short period, say five years or less.

Transfer Taxes.   In many jurisdictions transfer taxes are among
the largest expenses paid at closing. Some contract forms require
buyers to pay such taxes, others are more liberal and divide
transfer taxes equally between buyer and seller. Transfer taxes
should be regarded as a negotiable item, unless you find a form
that requires the seller to pay them.

20

Protecting Your Interests

Boilerplate agreements are written primarily to benefit sellers and brokers, an arrangement from which buyers are conspicuously absent. As a purchaser you can either accept the usual marketplace understandings or elect to defend your interests.

Defending your interests may be regarded by sellers and brokers as offensive, uncouth, unpleasant, and unnerving, but no one will suggest it's unfair. You have as much right to a good deal as sellers, something to emphasize if others forget.

A good deal is one where both parties benefit, but as a purchaser it's tough to get a fair bargain. Lacking experience, typically without training or representation, relying on form agreements that favor seller interests, it's easy to understand why first-time purchasers regard the homebuying process with apprehension.

Despite the barriers created by the traditional home marketing system, first-time buyers can do much to level the playing field. Study the market, learn about financing, check growth trends, look for homes where you can capture excess value, and you'll do much better than typical purchasers.

Yet the truth is that study and preparation by themselves are not enough. Like a college course, the final exam is critical and in real estate the final exam is represented by the sale agreement between buyers and sellers.

Will you pass the final? Without professional help—an attorney, buyer broker, or both—the chance of getting a good deal

157

drops with each boilerplate paragraph and standard clause you encounter.

Contract forms are designed so that, once signed, the deal is done and buyer and seller are committed to complete a transaction with specific terms, times, and consequences. If the contracting process was distinguished by some notion of equivalence, then iron-clad commitments might be attractive, but equivalence is the last quality found in real estate.

In the usual case, buyers can defend their interests by modifying form agreements and converting them into short-term options, options that evolve into binding contracts only under conditions satisfactory to purchasers. In effect, control of both the property and the deal shifts to buyers, at least for several days.

At a minimum, no purchase arrangement should be regarded as satisfactory without a financing clause. Such clauses provide that if a purchaser cannot get the exact financing shown in the form agreement, or financing that is otherwise satisfactory to the buyer, then the deal is off and the purchaser's deposit must be refunded in full.

What happens if a form agreement lacks a protective financing clause? In such cases buyers may face unappetizing alternatives: Either accept whatever mortgage rates and terms are available in the marketplace or pay damages for not going through with the deal.

In addition to a financing clause, first-time buyers will also want to make the deal dependent on a "satisfactory" home inspection.

Our list of experts (Chapter 16) included a home inspector, and now is the time to use one. A purchaser, for example, might say that the deal depends on the following conditions:

- First, a structural inspection of the property.
- Second, an inspector selected by the purchaser.
- Third, an inspection conducted within a reasonable time, say 10 business days.
- Fourth, a requirement that the inspection results are "satisfactory" in the purchaser's judgment.

- Fifth, a requirement that the deal shall be terminated and the buyer's deposit promptly refunded in full if the inspection is not viewed as "satisfactory" by the purchaser.

A correctly written structural inspection converts a one-sided, iron-clad form agreement into an option that gives purchasers time to examine the property and decide whether or not to buy it. Coincidentally, a correctly written structural inspection also ties up the property so that it cannot be sold to anyone else until the purchaser has made a decision.

Will a seller accept a structural inspection? Some sellers will refuse any offer that modifies a standardized form agreement, a position that typically softens if a property remains unsold for a lengthy period. Other sellers, and their brokers, will encourage structural inspections to prevent future litigation. Their reasoning works like this: By hiring an independent inspector a buyer cannot later claim to have relied only on the seller or broker for structural advice.

Structural inspections are keenly important because few first-time buyers are qualified to judge a home's physical aspects. A good inspector will check electrical, heating, air-conditioning, and plumbing systems; basements and attics for dryness and damage; all appliances, roofs and gutters, fireplaces and chimneys; and even TV antennas.

A structural inspection will find faults with the property. Most will be inconsequential, but for buyers serious questions can arise if costly problems are uncovered. If you find that the roof leaks and needs to be replaced in two years, do you go through with the deal, or do you say the property's condition can only be viewed as "satisfactory" if the seller is willing to replace the roof or provide a credit for repairs, perhaps $3,500? Now the seller must make decisions. Does the seller make the repairs you require, or does the he or she look for another purchaser?

A buyer's perception of "satisfactory" will certainly be influenced by the local real estate market. If prices are rising and sales are hot, getting additional concessions from a seller will be difficult and a demand for repairs can cause the deal to fail. Conversely, if sales are slow, sellers may be eager to finalize the deal.

During the time available to conduct the inspection, a first-time buyer will surely want to examine both the property and the deal with great care. As part of the examination process, be certain to accompany the inspector as he goes through the property. Ask questions as you go and take pictures.

You want photographs because they show how the property looked at the time you bought it. If there is damage between the time the contract is accepted and the date of settlement, photos can show the property's prior condition and establish the seller's obligation to make repairs.

If you're the buyer and a deal depends on your satisfaction, then it's difficult if not impossible for anyone else to define the term. Your vision of satisfaction may not match anyone else's, but you're the judge and jury. Even if a property is in wonderful condition, it may not be satisfactory if your goal is to find a property that's ripe for renovation.

Not only can you make deals dependent on satisfactory structural inspections, there can also be tests for electric wiring, legal reviews, surveys, roof repairs, termite damage, leaky basements, kitchen appliances, clothes washers, or just about anything else that is in, near, or part of a house.

As a practical matter you only need one clause that depends on satisfaction to create an option. An attorney can write and attach such language to a basic contract form, language that takes precedence over any conflicting or contrary wording found in the original document and assures the return of your complete deposit if you are not satisfied.

ESCROW ACCOUNTS

Even the smoothest deals often run into problems because of weather or other factors over which buyers and sellers have no control.

If you live in Boston and buy the Hudson property in January, no one can tell if the air-conditioning system works. The issue here is not that someone is at fault, but that you cannot tell if the system is in good working order, or working at all. Instead of finding out in May and possibly facing a $2,000 bill to replace the entire system, it makes sense to shift the repair burden to seller Hudson through the use of an escrow fund.

Escrow funds are created by taking cash from the seller at closing and holding the money in an account. For example, if the contract is properly written, or if a "satisfactory" structural inspection requires it, you can demand that seller Hudson place $2,000 in an escrow account held by the settlement provider to assure that the air-conditioning system is in *good* working order. If the system doesn't work, or if it needs to be replaced, you then have $2,000 available to underwrite such expenses.

Escrow accounts can be created to assure that promised work is completed, that repairs take place, and that replacements and improvements are made by a certain date. A proper escrow account will have these elements:

- Money placed in escrow will be available for a limited purpose, perhaps to fix the air conditioner but not the roof or the oven.

- The fund will be held for a limited time. If an inspection is not conducted by a given date, then escrow account funds must be returned to the seller.

- The seller or the seller's representative should be present when a test or examination is required before escrow funds are used. If money is set aside to assure that the heating system works, then someone from the seller's side of the deal should be there when the system is turned on.

- The escrow fund should pay interest. The interest should go to the seller unless required for repairs.

- The escrow fund should be established and maintained by the party conducting settlement.

Given a choice between strong verbal promises, powerful oaths, and absolute sincerity, or the comfort of money in the bank, first-time buyers would be wise to insist on the creation of an escrow fund to assure the completion of promised work and as a hedge against potential repair bills.

21

Contracting for Condos and Co-Ops

To most people buying "real estate" means buying land and a residence. To lawyers, brokers, and lenders, real estate is something more, possibly land and a perhaps a residence but always an array of rights and privileges. The distinctions made by real estate professionals should interest first-time buyers because they affect your ability to buy, finance, and sell property.

Fee simple is the highest and best form of real estate ownership. It means you own property outright—the land, the house, the fence, the garage, everything. You can rent it, rent part of it, paint it orange, and have pets. If oil or gold are discovered under your lot, you can sell the mineral rights. Pay your mortgage, pay your taxes, and the property is yours. You are the ruler of all that has been surveyed.

Lenders like fee simple real estate because it's an easy matter to identify the property and attach a lien. If you don't pay the mortgage, the lender gets the property. Brokers like fee simple real estate because it's easy to list, show, and market.

The trouble is, not all real estate is fee simple property, especially real estate purchased by first-time buyers. First-timers often purchase condominiums, properties where the buyer owns a unit as well as an interest in common areas such as sidewalks, tennis courts, and pools.

Condos are attractive to first-time buyers because when condominiums and fee simple property are available in equivalent areas, condos tend to be less expensive.

Condos are cheaper because they are most often in the form of townhouses and apartment-style flats, attached housing with less interior space and therefore less cost. Compared to detached housing, more units can be built per acre so land costs per unit are lower. Common walls and facilities save additional dollars. Building many units at once produces economies of scale that can be passed through to purchasers.

Not every economic measure favors condos, however. Own a condominium and there is a monthly condo fee to pay, perhaps $5 or perhaps several hundred dollars, depending on the services and benefits received.

As to financing, condos raise two issues. First, lenders will count condo fees when they compute PITI. Pay $86 per month in condo fees and you have $86 less for principal, interest, taxes, and insurance.

Second, many lenders will not make condo loans. Others will only make loans to "approved" condos such as those which qualify for FHA financing. If a project has not been approved by a lender, then would-be purchasers must pay several hundred dollars to have various condo documents reviewed by the lender's attorney.

Lenders check condo papers because such documents influence condo values and therefore the ability to borrow. In turn, *first-time buyers should always condition condo purchase offers on a satisfactory review of the condo's declaration, by-laws, rules and regulations, and budget.* If the review is not satisfactory to you, make certain your offer provides that the deal is off and that your deposit will be returned in full.

Unlike fee simple property, buying a condo allows a condominium association to raise or lower monthly fees, conduct or defer maintenance, or close the pool on Tuesdays. Condo associations can also interfere in areas which no fee simple owner would tolerate. For example, there have been battles between individual owners and condo associations over such issues as appropriate doorway colors and the right to erect a flagpole.

Condo documents will tell you how votes are apportioned (one vote per unit, or votes based on unit size), whether a reserve fund has been established for emergency repairs, if rentals are restricted (and how they are restricted), and if pets are allowed.

In addition to reviewing documents, first-time buyers should speak to condo association officials, especially treasurers. You want to know if a condo fee increase is planned or anticipated, and you also want to know if a "special" assessment is scheduled or likely.

Special assessments become necessary when condos lack reserves to pay irregular expenses. For instance, if a condo has 50 units and collects $10 per month for a reserve fund, then at year's end the reserve fund will hold $6,000 ($10 × 12 × 50). If repairing leaky roofs will cost $20,000, then the reserve will be wiped out and each unit owner will face a $280 special assessment ($20,000 less $6,000 leaves $14,000; $14,000 divided by 50 units equals $280).

Not only do special assessments cost money, they must be paid. Neglect to pay a special assessment and the amount owed becomes a lien against the property and unpaid liens can lead to foreclosure. Since condo associations determine if special assessments are necessary, and since condo associations can determine how much unit owners must "contribute" when special assessments are required, it's easy to understand why first-time buyers should look at condo finances with care.

Even among those lenders who do make condo loans, many stay away from projects with a high proportion of investors, say 25 to 30 percent of all units. When investors own many units, lenders often refuse to finance deals unless purchasers put down at least 25 percent. In some cases, lenders simply refuse to make loans to such projects.

You're not an investor, but since lender rules relate to condo projects rather than individual units, *the decision by other unit owners to rent can reduce the value and salability of your property.* In comparison, if you own a fee simple property and several houses on the block are rented, lenders are not likely to invoke special rules.

In addition to condos, first-time buyers may consider buying property in a *planned unit development,* or PUD. A PUD can be seen as a large property, perhaps an entire "new town" with detached homes, condo townhouses, and apartment-style condos as well as pools, bike paths, and recreation centers.

A well-planned and plausible PUD can be a good candidate for future growth, development, and appreciation. As the PUD develops, as more facilities are built and a sense of community is established, property values can increase at rates equal to or better than area houses.

Cooperatives are another housing concept often embraced by first-time purchasers. Buy a co-op and you become a shareholder in a corporation that owns property. You also own the right to use a particular unit and you have an interest in common assets such as hallways and tennis courts.

While co-ops may be a housing concept, they are not a direct form of real estate ownership. Having corporate stock means you can be outvoted at any time, a possibility not faced by fee simple owners.

Lenders will finance and refinance co-op projects because the loan is secured by the entire property, a good system for lenders but not so good for individual buyers. If a project has 50 units, borrows $5 million, and 10 unit owners do not make required monthly payments, all 50 units secure the loan and therefore all 50 units can be foreclosed—including units owned by people who have made full and timely payments.

Assuming that all 50 units are the same size, each started out with an underlying debt of $100,000 ($5 million divided by 50).

If co-op values increase, if values rise to $150,000 per unit, then a buyer cannot simply go out and get a new loan. The unit is already pledged as security for the underlying mortgage. A buyer must come up with the difference between the unit's market value ($150,000) and the remaining mortgage balance ($100,000).

Since most buyers do not want to put down 33 percent, since most first-time buyers do not have $50,000 in cash, and since $50,000 is enough money to buy a more expensive detached home, four realistic options remain open.

First, the price can be reduced, an approach that sellers will find unappealing.

Second, the seller can take back some or all of the financing needed to close the deal.

Third, some lenders will provide re-sale financing if they have a *recognition agreement* with the co-op project, essentially second trusts that help bridge the gap between selling prices and underlying mortgages. Lenders who offer recognition financing will do so only because they have negotiated special concessions with the co-op corporation.

Fourth, there is a growing movement to provide *share financing,* second trusts that can be re-sold in the secondary market. Between the underlying mortgage and share financing, as much as 90 percent of the entire purchase price can be financed. For information, write to the National Cooperative Bank, attention Share Loan Services, 1630 Connecticut Avenue NW, Washington, DC 20009.

First-time buyers should approach co-op buying with the same care used to acquire any real estate. Deals should be contingent not only on your satisfaction with the unit, but also the co-op's incorporation papers, budget, rules, and other documents.

When considering co-ops understand that an "owner" cannot freely sell his or her unit. Your ability to purchase will be tied to acceptance by a co-op board that may or may not agree to the sale, based on whatever standards board members elect to employ.

The good news is that if your offer is accepted, transfer costs are minimal in most jurisdictions. Ownership is represented by stock and stock is easy to buy, sell, and trade when compared to direct real estate interests.

LAND LEASES

With fee simple property, owners can sell some or all of their many rights. In some areas owners have elected to lease their ground for a lengthy period, perhaps 75 or 99 years. A project is then erected on the ground and those who lease the property pay an annual ground rent.

Although ground leases are typically used with commercial buildings in major downtown areas, there are residential projects built on leased land. The argument for such properties is that because purchasers are not buying ground, it's possible to acquire a real estate interest at less cost.

The obvious arguments against ground leases are that those who lease must pay annual ground rents and that ground rents are likely to escalate over time. In addition, when the lease or any extensions expire, all property improvements revert to the land holder.

22

New Homes

Nearly 1 million new homes are sold each year and many are bought by first-time purchasers. New homes offer the latest styles, the most recent construction concepts, warranties, modern appliances, and the chance for buyers to create their own environment from scratch.

New homes are typically marketed from model units carefully designed to be light, airy, and spacious. Skillfully prepared by professional decorators, new home models often feature the best available appliances, fireplaces, finished rec rooms, skylights, carpets, and wallpaper.

New home buyers commonly make this major purchase on the basis of a model, a floor plan, a site map, and the developer's contract. In many instances the home itself is represented by a dot on a map—a home tomorrow but today a pile of lumber, pipes, and wires that are not up, not complete, and not subject to the scrutiny first-time buyers normally crave.

To some extent the concerns facing new home buyers are the same as those facing people who purchase existing properties. Both groups want a great location, the best possible house, the most advantageous financing, and a property that represents good value over many years. And although both new and existing homes can provide the benefits sought by first-time purchasers, the buying process for each type of property is different.

For instance, existing-home sellers are unlikely to print their own sales agreement. Developers, in contrast, commonly produce their own custom-made and neatly printed forms. Such forms are frequently inventive and ingenious. Whether builder sale agreements also balance the interests between builder and buyer is a question that can only be answered on a case-by-case basis.

Part of the problem is that building is an inexact art. Because construction can be delayed by bad weather, material shipments, and labor shortages, precise settlement dates are often not met.

Without a precise settlement date, buyers may be unable to notify landlords that they intend to vacate rental property at a particular time. Not being able to provide advance notice to landlords may mean that purchasers pay extra rent, forfeit deposits, or both. Paying to lock in a loan may not make sense, because construction problems can delay closing until after a lock-in has expired.

The financing problem can sometimes be solved by obtaining a loan through the builder or through a mortgage company owned by the developer. To be worthwhile, such financing must offer competitive rates and terms that can be locked in *until closing*, whenever closing occurs. If rates and terms are guaranteed until closing, builders have a considerable incentive to complete units, especially when interest rates are rising.

Sales agreements for new homes, like sales agreements for existing properties, can contain boilerplate language that homebuyers should avoid. Here are selected issues that should concern first-time buyers:

Closing.   Form agreements used by developers will sometimes stipulate that the purchaser can select the settlement provider, but only with the builder's approval. This innocuous language can allow the builder to require the use of a particular lawyer or title company, parties likely to have a strong business relationship with the developer.

Escrow.   A builder's form agreement may provide that even if work is not complete by closing, no funds can be escrowed to assure that promised tasks are finished. Without money set aside to guarantee completion, buyers must depend on the builder's goodwill for repairs.

Price.   Buyers want to know all costs in advance and that quoted prices will not change.

Some new home agreements guarantee prices and allow the purchaser to assign the contract. In such cases, if new home prices rise, it may be possible to sell the contract before closing and pocket the price increase for yourself.

Structural Inspections.   The use of a structural inspector with new homes is essential, since the seller is absolutely familiar with construction matters while the buyer is not.

Final inspections are typically held just before closing. The builder's representative and the buyer tour the property and incomplete, missing, or broken items are entered onto a *punch list.* The builder is then supposed to correct any defects noted on the punch list after closing.

Conflicts can arise at several points in the inspection process.

First, reserve enough time to complete the inspection. An inspection at 10 A.M. followed by closing 14 miles away at noon may not leave enough time for a thorough job.

Second, check the punch list as you go through the property to assure that each item is entered.

Third, do not agree to an inspection if utilities are not working. Some builders have been known to schedule inspections when the electricity is off. It is then impossible to know if appliances work, if plugs are correctly installed, or if the service box is properly wired. Some builders also limit electrical warranties to defects found at the walk-through, so if the electricity is off there will be few defects to find.

Fourth, bring a structural inspector with you. You may not be a construction expert, but the inspector is. The inspector will know what is up to code and what isn't, what should be on the punch list, and what additional work is required.

Substitution.   Builders may reserve the right to update plans or to substitute materials. Such clauses can be benign, but in a literal sense they can give builders the right to change any aspect of the project.

Title Insurance.   New homes are often constructed on large tracts under a system where developers first secure the right to subdivide and build, and then buy individual lots as each house is sold. With this system, developers are not forced to buy the entire property at once or to pay heavy interest costs until the project is sold out.

To make this system work, there must be a title search for the entire property. Then, when you buy, there is another title search for your lot to assure that you and your lender do not face unknown liens. Since there was a recent title search it may be possible to get a new search at the "re-issue" rate for your lot, especially if the individual who conducts closing is also the person who did the developer's title work.

NEW HOME BARGAINS

There's a natural and obvious conflict between homebuyers and homebuilders. Homebuilders want the best possible prices for their property and buyers want to pay less. So how can first-time buyers get better deals?

Buy Early. If the first units in a project sell quickly, then prices for later sections are likely to climb. Having "sold" signs on the site plan allows builders to show would-be purchasers that their project is successful. In effect, early buyers can often find lower prices because builders want to create a positive sales environment.

Contract for Models. Builders first erect and then furnish model homes, homes that reflect the builder's best efforts. Such models are expensive, so builders are happy to play the sell-and-rent game. It works like this:

The builder finds a buyer (or a buyer contacts the builder) and offers to sell model units for a given price. The builder also agrees to rent the unit back from the purchaser for a specific period, anywhere from 6 to 24 months. After the lease period is over, the property reverts to the owner who can live in it, sell it, or rent it.

Buying a model house may resolve a major financial problem for first-time purchasers. Because lenders want the builder's business, and because the property will have a written lease, financing is easily available. From your perspective as a buyer, you have arguably purchased the project's best property at an early price, there's a lease that covers monthly costs, and because the property is rented, you can obtain substantial tax write-offs.

In some instances, the developer owns a mortgage company and the company will provide financing. Such deals can be extremely profitable because the developer makes money selling the model, plus there are fees and charges to be earned from the loan. From the buyer's perspective, model homes can offer attractive financing, a guaranteed tenant, delayed occupancy, and the possibility of appreciation.

Buying a model home is not worthwhile for those who need to move quickly. Also, care must be taken to assure that both buyer and builder understand what happens when the lease is finished. For example, what are the builder's obligations to clean the property? Is the builder required to hook up appliances and add the interior doors that are usually missing in model homes? Should the office area remain, or should it be converted into a garage, rec room, or other residential space? If not yet installed, will a driveway be added?

Hidden Discounts.   It is difficult to bargain with large builders because they typically have the financial strength to hold prices over a lengthy period. But holding property is not the builder's goal and to move units builders in slow markets will often give hidden discounts.

The builder does not want to sell property at discounted prices, so rather than lower prices, the builder instead changes the package being sold. To the outside world it looks as though the builder has asked and is getting a particular price for his property, say $100,000 per unit. In reality, to make a sale the builder offers a more valuable package, the property plus upgrades such as better appliances or a higher grade of carpeting.

Down Markets.   Building is a tough business, especially when local housing markets are tight and prices are steady or falling. In such an environment a builder can have excess units that are expensive to maintain. Rather than pay high monthly costs, the builder may elect to sell the units at "low" prices.

Whether such properties are a good deal will depend on individual situations. If the units are part of a project and money has not been set aside to assure the completion of amenities, then it's possible that the promised pool and other features will never be built and that the units will remain perpetually unattractive. Also, if there are construction problems with the unit and the builder is no longer in business, who do you call for repairs?

Conversely, in completed projects that have amenities in place, buying at discount can be a good deal, especially if the local economy turns around and values once again begin to rise.

Last Units.   The final units sold by builders are often the most profitable because earlier sales have covered all costs and the developer is now flush with success (to say nothing of cash). A few unsold units also means that the sales office must be maintained, advertising continued, and carrying costs paid out. Rather than fool with such expenses, some builders will offer either close-out discounts or upgrades to unload final units. Since final units may also reflect higher prices than earlier units, builders can afford to be more flexible.

23

Closing

After finding, financing, and contracting for a house, homeownership is surely within sight. Whether it's also within reach is another question.

Once a sales contract has been accepted, buyers have an equitable property interest. Not title and not ownership, but a clear interest and claim in the property, an interest that is real and in some cases an interest which actually can be sold.

To go from an equitable interest to full ownership it's necessary to finalize the homebuying process. Clean up the details and you too can be a homeowner.

The "details" can be found in the sales agreement. If you promised to apply for financing within ten days, that's a detail. If the seller is obligated to paint the dining room, that too is a detail.

One major detail concerns financing. You must make application for financing, usually within seven to ten days after the contract is finally ratified. Buyers who do not apply within the stated period can lose their deposits.

To obtain a loan and to satisfy possible contract requirements you want to meet with lenders as soon as possible. Since loan officers schedule appointments at nights and on weekends, applying for a loan need not interfere with your normal business routine.

Not only do you want to apply for a loan, you want a lender's letter showing that you appear to qualify for financing. Such qualification letters are often required by sellers, but equally important they show that you met with a lender on a particular date, completed a loan application, paid a loan application fee, and did in fact apply for financing as you promised.

Once a lender is selected and you've applied for a loan, it's then your job to remain in contact with the loan officer and to supply whatever information or documentation is required. Having documents assembled at application will make the entire lending process easier, quicker, and less stressful.

You will want to work with the lender, the seller, and the seller's broker or brokers to assure that the property is open and available for an appraisal, termite inspection, structural inspection, and other examinations. As a matter of courtesy, brokers should arrange such appointments, but as a buyer you have an obligation to select inspectors and to make certain that each check is timely. For example, if you have ten days to examine the property and the broker schedules an inspection on the eleventh day, without a written contract modification or an earlier inspection date you may lose valuable rights. (See Table 34.)

Depending on where you live, closing may be handled by an attorney, title company, or escrow company. The important point is that you pay a fee for this service and someone else does the work. It's not necessary to be a settlement expert to close a sale, even if you buy from a self-seller.

The settlement provider will tell you what papers are needed by closing and what steps must be taken to complete the deal. First-time buyers should ask:

- Who is responsible for a title search and abstract?

- Who will provide title insurance?

- Must the termite inspection be paid before closing (in which case you will need a receipt), or can it be paid at settlement (in which case the settlement provider will pay the fee and you will pay more at closing to cover this expense)?

- Must the property insurance policy be paid and delivered to the lender prior to settlement, or can a paid-in-full policy be brought to closing? This is an issue to double-check with the lender.

Table 34   BASIC SETTLEMENT CHECKLIST

What is the closing date? _____

What time is closing? _____

Who will conduct closing?

    Name: _____

    Phone: _____

Where will closing be held? _____

Who will conduct a title search? _____

Who will contact the gas company? _____

Who will contact the electric company? _____

Who will contact the water company? _____

Who will contact other utilities? _____

When must a paid-up property insurance policy be delivered?

_____

When must a termite inspection be delivered? _____

When is the walk-through scheduled? _____

What repairs must be completed by closing? _____

How much cash is required at closing? _____

What form of check will be accepted at closing? _____

- Are there any other papers that must be delivered to the lender before closing or that should be brought to settlement?

- Who is responsible for reading meters and assuring that you are not billed for the seller's gas, electric, and water usage?

Utility matters should be handled with care. Most utilities are well organized when it comes time to change service from one user to another, but as a practical matter utility workers need time to read meters and change billing codes.

Not changing utility bills promptly can create massive problems. If the seller discontinues electric service as of closing and it's January in New Jersey, there's an excellent probability that unless action is quickly taken, pipes will freeze and the property may not be habitable—experiences you want to avoid.

Also, it should be said that water bills in many areas are a lien against the property. The settlement provider in such areas will have the meter read and pay such bills to assure that all back claims against the property are removed.

- How much cash will be required at settlement to close the deal? Under the Real Estate Settlement and Procedures Act (RESPA), final figures are supposed to be available to you 24 hours before settlement so that, in theory, if you think closing costs are too high you can schedule settlement with someone else and obtain a different loan.

- How should the money be paid (by certified check, cashiers check, a large wad of bills, etc.)?

- What tax forms, if any, must be filed? In some states property used as a prime residence may qualify for a homeowner's tax exemption, depending on your income. It may be necessary to file certain papers at closing to obtain such benefits.

If you have been working with an attorney and the attorney is conducting settlement, the process should be both easy and friendly. If closing is being handled by another party, then have your attorney, or buyer broker, raise questions and find answers.

Buyers often ask if it's necessary to have their attorney attend closing. In general the answer is no, providing that your lawyer reviews all final settlement papers prior to closing and that no disputes with the seller are anticipated.

WALK-THROUGHS

Prior to settlement buyers are entitled to walk through the property. As a purchaser you want nothing more than to assure that the property is being delivered in the condition promised by the seller. If the property is to be broom clean, then the house should be entirely devoid of trash and old furniture. If an old car was to be removed from the backyard, it should be gone. If the appliances worked when the contract was ratified, they should work now.

With a new property you will want to go through the house with the builder's representative and your inspector. Items that are incomplete, incorrect, or not done at all should be marked on the builder's punch list. For your protection, maintain your own list of faulty items and make certain that every questionable item is entered onto the builder's punch sheet. At the end of the walk-through, compare your list with the builder's to assure they are identical.

Buyers should insist that all seller obligations are satisfied, and if they are not satisfied buyers should then demand suitable compensation. For instance, if a repair is not made, then a liberal amount from the seller should be placed in escrow to assure completion.

DISPUTES

Closings are sometimes vile events where buyers and sellers scream back and forth. But if the contract is clear and well written, if everyone understands their obligations and performs as promised, then settlement should be a quick, tidy, and quiet experience.

If you feel a dispute is likely, then bring your attorney or buyer broker to closing. Be prepared to show exactly where the contract requires something of the seller and have a sane remedy in mind.

Remember, the goal is not to see which participant can yell the loudest or destroy the most furniture. Instead, describe the problem politely ("The contract does say that the seller will replace the old dishwasher with a Dish-Delight 408") and suggest a remedy that the seller can accept ("We understand that the required replacement was not made and all we ask is to set aside enough money to assure the promised work").

If the debate becomes personal, if buyers and sellers simply hate one another, then it can make sense to have each party sign appropriate papers at separate times or in separate rooms. The obligation to close is then satisfied without physical contact or as much emotional travail.

OCCUPANCY AND DECORATOR AGREEMENTS

Closing dates often denote a specific moment when ownership is supposed to change hands. Sometimes, however, while title is transferred, occupancy is not.

It can happen that the sellers wish to remain on the property after closing, a desire that may be attractive to buyers. If you need more time in your present location, then having sellers who want to stay can be a blessing.

Certainly you will want to charge an occupancy fee, perhaps something equal to your cost for principal, interest, taxes, and insurance. Certainly, also, you will want the seller to pay utilities and maintain the property in good condition.

If the sellers wish to stay for a limited period, then any *post-settlement occupancy arrangement* with them should be in writing and should offer all the protections local landlords require, including a large deposit.

Buyers should be certain that:

- The sellers carry insurance for their goods while you carry fire, theft, and liability coverage.

- The sellers' occupancy is seen as an accommodation between buyers and sellers, not as a rental agreement. If the property is "rented," then rent control rules may apply. (Rent control rules may apply anyway, depending on local regulations.)

- The sellers' occupancy is short because the new mortgage lender may require buyer/borrowers to move in within a specific time, say 30 days. Alternatively, it may be possible to obtain financing with an understanding that the seller will stay on the property for two months, or three months, or whatever amount of time is appropriate. If the lender agrees to a delayed occupancy, always obtain the lender's approval in writing.

It's also possible that the situation can be reversed, that you wish to occupy the property prior to closing, what is known as a *pre-settlement occupancy arrangement.*

If the property is vacant some sellers will simply allow you to move in early. Smarter sellers will require a written agreement so they receive an occupancy fee and you pay for insurance and utilities.

A more likely scenario works like this: You don't want to move in but you would like to paint and fix up. If the property is empty, why not?

In this situation, sellers are likely to want a pre-settlement decorator agreement, a contract which allows the buyer to paint and repair the property but not to occupy it. Such agreements routinely call for the buyer to pay all utilities and sometimes to pay a weekly fee.

Occupancy and decorator agreements are often easy to obtain before closing because they routinely have a "got ya" clause. Such forms routinely provide that in exchange for early access, not only will buyers pay a fee and underwrite utility costs, but that purchasers also accept the property in "as is" condition. In effect, such wording may mean that in exchange for early access to the property, your right to demand repairs and warranty work will be lost or limited.

As an alternative, buyers may prefer to build occupancy and decorator clauses into the basic sales contract. It's easier to plan ahead and say that, as a sale condition, "the Purchaser shall be allowed to paint and repair subject property at Purchaser's expense during the 30-day period prior to settlement's scheduled date." If the property is not occupied, or the seller strongly wants to sell, such bland language may be acceptable. It may be one-sided, but then so are form agreements where buyers are expected to waive important rights.

24

Warranties

The homebuying process is marked with uncertainty and conflict, but nowhere is there more uncertainty or more potential for conflict than when the deal is done and the property is yours. Now if something goes wrong, citizen homeowner, the problem is yours. Or is it?

A home is not only a place to live, it's also a product designed to accomplish a specific purpose. And in our society we have decided that when products used for their intended purpose within a given time span do not perform as promised, those who make and sell such products can be held responsible.

How much responsibility and who might be accountable depend largely on warranties, guarantees found in every real estate deal.

One form of guarantee is the *implied warranty,* an unwritten understanding that a house is a house and that as a house it should be habitable, free from faulty materials, and finished in a "good and workmanlike" manner.

Rules that effectively grant guarantees can be created by government regulation. So-called *imposed warranties* can require that homes meet building codes and zoning ordinances. In New York state, for example, there is an implied warranty for "housing merchants." Under the New York program, new home buyers are protected against material defects for six years. Plumbing, electrical, heating, cooling, and ventilation systems must be warranted for two years. There's also a one-year work-manship guarantee.

Express warranties are a third form of protection. Express warranties are written promises, the value of which depends on how they are written, how long they last, and someone's willing-ness—such as a builder, seller, or manufacturer—to make repairs and improvements if something goes wrong.

Warranties are complex, but first-time buyers should consider these basic points:

First, new homes and re-sale properties are not necessarily covered by the same warranty rules. New homes are typically protected by imposed and implied warranties, while existing homes have less coverage.

Second, in addition to warranties from builders and owners, buyers may also benefit from appliance warranties.

Third, there are limited warranty programs for both new and existing homes.

Existing home buyers can often get limited warranties through realty brokers that offer one-year protection against major defects. The precise terms and conditions vary, and typi-cally there is a deductible if a claim is made. A willingness by sellers or their brokers to buy warranty protection as an induce-ment to purchase can be valuable.

If *you* are interested in buying such protection, ask these questions:

- How much does the policy cost?
- How long will it last?
- How large is the deductible?
- Other than the deductible and the initial premium, will you face any additional costs? For instance, is there a fee to "inves-tigate" claims?
- What, exactly, is covered by the policy and what is not cov-ered?
- What is the maximum coverage amount under the policy?

As to new homes, they typically offer more valuable warran-ties than existing units. Furnaces, hot water heaters, central air conditioners, stoves, refrigerators, clothes washers, clothes dryers, dishwashers, and disposals are all new and all likely to be covered under manufacturer warranties. With such warranties, buyers should have few initial repair costs, if any.

In addition to manufacturer warranties, builders may also guarantee their work. Such warranties are only as good as the builder's commitment to make repairs, which in some cases is very good.

As an alternative to direct builder guarantees, limited warranties are also available through outside parties. The largest protection program is operated by the Home Owners Warranty Corporation (HOW). To date, more than two million new homes have been enrolled under the HOW plan.

What should you look for in a home warranty program? Here are the basic issues to consider.

Is it a "warranty" or a "limited warranty"? Builders and just about everyone else will provide limited warranties so that the liability to make repairs and pay claims is not open-ended. Since virtually all warranties are limited, the real issue concerns just how much coverage is offered. Warranties for some products are so limited that they offer little practical protection against defects.

What is covered? A "protection" plan that excludes or greatly limits coverage may not be valuable. For instance, suppose electrical problems discovered during the walk-through are covered. That's good news if there are no difficulties or if a problem is found. But what happens if the electrical system shorts out two days after you move in? Or, what if every outlet was not checked during the brief walk-through process and it turns out that several are defective? Now—despite a warranty—you have no protection.

At the very least, a limited warranty program should cover basic mechanical systems—water, electrical, heat, and air conditioning—as well as all related devices, controls, wires, pipes, valves, and ducts for at least a year.

Another item to consider up front is workmanship. Pieces of a house should not fall off, basements should not flood, large fissures should not develop in concrete, etc. If a builder is unwilling to cover workmanship for at least a year, then you should seriously wonder if the property you are buying represents anything other than temporary housing.

As time passes, homes are influenced by normal wear and tear and therefore warranty coverage should become less extensive. But wear and tear should not instantly damage wiring, plumbing, or ductwork. Delivery systems should be expected to hold up for more than a year and so should have longer coverage, say at least two years.

A third construction category concerns major structural defects. The roof should not sag and a chimney should not fall over. A house, by its nature, should be sufficiently well built that you need not worry about such problems for a long time, 10 years at least.

What guidelines are used? Warranty protection can be a matter of debate when coverage is not well defined. For instance, is every concrete crack covered under a warranty? Hairline cracks may not represent a problem, but what about a crack that measures an eighth of an inch across? To some builders such cracks are just part of the normal settling process. To others, a crack that broad requires repair and such repairs should be a warranty item.

If someone offers a limited warranty, then ask for a list of standards showing exactly what is covered and what is not protected.

Does the policy transfer if you sell the property? If so, at what cost? As a home buyer it is probable that you will not own your property for 30 years. If you sell in 10 years or less, then the benefits of a new home warranty should convey to the second owners. The ability to transfer protection is attractive for three reasons. First, an existing warranty can be a valuable sales tool. Second, an existing warranty can protect the buyer if a major defect turns up. Third, a new home warranty can be combined with a short-term re-sale warranty to provide a broad range of coverage.

Is there a premium? A new-home limited warranty is an inducement to buy from a given builder. Since the builder wants you to buy the property, let him or her pay for the warranty.

Is there a deductible? Insurance coverage, whether for medical claims, auto protection, or new homes, is less costly when insurors need not worry about small claims. Since a home is a big-ticket item, it follows that warranty coverage will not extend to missing bolts or a faucet washer. Look for a reasonable deductible, say $250. In the context of a home, $250 is not an unreasonable amount.

Is there an inspection fee or any other charge in the event of a claim? Always ask for a written statement outlining your costs in the event of a claim. For example, if there is a $250 deductible and a $150 inspection fee or other cost to investigate a claim, then each claim will cost the homeowner at least $400 ($250 plus $150) before the warranty organization will pay a dime.

How are disputes with a builder resolved? A warranty program should assume that a home is a complex product and that disputes with builders and developers will arise from time to time. If there are problems a process should be in place which allows disputes to be resolved as quickly and inexpensively as possible.

On a rational basis, the process should first require that buyer and builder try to work out their problems directly. Next, if a voluntary agreement isn't possible, the matter should be arbitrated and the arbitration agreement should be binding on the builder. If the owner is not happy with arbitration, then the option to take the matter to court should be open. As a practical matter, arbitration should resolve most problems.

What happens if the builder goes out of business? Some projects are built by single-purpose corporate developers or builders, corporations that are established to complete only one project. Once the project is over, the corporation is shut down. One-shot corporations are fine, except that homebuyers must then wonder who they pursue if they have a problem and the builder is out of business. The warranty firm should be able (and required) to step in when the builder no longer exists, has gone bankrupt, or refuses to abide by an arbitration decision.

Appendix A

Glossary

By its nature the homebuying process is mysterious, complicated, and confused. All deals are different, and yet each is held together by words and phrases which are clearly understood by real estate insiders.

To be an equal in the homebuying process, and to understand events as they unfold, you must know the basic words, phrases, and ideas which guide the real estate business. If you don't, then you are likely to pay more for the home you buy and to get less value for each dollar you spend. Here are three quick examples:

- An owner will sell a home to Forbes at a discounted price if Forbes will accept a quit-claim deed. Sounds okay—if one deed is as good as another. But there are many types of deeds and it is entirely possible that a quit-claim deed has no value at all.

- In addition to a first trust from a regular lender, Trenton needs additional financing to buy his first home. When seller Adkins offers to provide a "10-year second trust for $20,000 with a three-year balloon," Trenton is excited. Trenton likes the low monthly payments, but he doesn't understand that in three years the note will end and he will be obligated to pay Adkins nearly $20,000 at one time, a balloon payment Trenton is unlikely to have.

- The Johnsons liked the Woodmont house and offered to buy it, but only if there was a structural inspection. Woodmont agreed and the contract said that "Purchasers shall have the right to have a structural inspection by an inspector of their choice and at Purchasers' expense within ten days of ratification." But what happens if the inspector finds a leaking roof, rotted floors, and a broken hot water heater? The words in the contract do not say that the inspection had to be "satisfactory" to the Johnsons or the deal was off. The clause also did not say the Johnson's deposit would be returned if the inspection was unacceptable.

First-time buyers should know real estate's phrases and expressions, not only dictionary-style definitions, but also insights, values, and perceptions. Here is a basic list of important words and phrases that every first-time buyer should know.

Acceptance. A positive response to an offer or counter-offer. There are conditional acceptances ("I'll accept if you'll pay another $1,500 for the property"), express or written acceptances, implied acceptances ("I'm not going to say anything if you move in early"), and qualified acceptances ("I'll accept your offer subject to my lawyer liking the deal").

Addenda. Clauses, documents, or statements added to a contract that alter it in some way. To be enforceable, addenda must be signed or initialed by both buyer and seller and clearly referenced in the contract. For example, a contract might refer to addenda by saying that "Addenda are attached to and made a part of this contract."

Addendum. Singular of *addenda.*

Agent. Has two meanings in real estate. First, in general terms, someone who acts on behalf of another for a fee, such as a real estate broker or an attorney. Second, a type of real estate licensee who works under the authority of a real estate broker.

Amortization. As payments are made to a lender each month the mortgage debt, or principal, declines in most cases. This process is called amortization. Also, see SELF-AMORTIZATION and NEGATIVE AMORTIZATION.

Amortization Schedule. A chart showing how each monthly payment is divided into principal and interest during the loan term and how much principal remains after each payment. For a level-payment, 30-year, $100,000 loan at 10 percent interest, monthly payments will be $877.57 and an amortization schedule would look like this:

Payment	Interest	Principal	Balance
#1	$833.33	$44.24	$99,955.76
#2	$832.96	$44.61	$99,911.15
#3	$832.59	$44.98	$99,866.17
#4	$832.22	$45.35	$99,820.82
etc.			

Annual Percentage Rate (APR). The true rate of interest for a loan over its projected life, say 30 years. May be different than the initial interest rate or the nominal interest rate before compounding.

Appraisal. An estimate of value produced by an independent appraiser. Typically based on such factors as replacement cost, past sales of like properties, and the ability to produce income.

Appraiser. A person familiar with local real estate values who estimates the worth of particular properties. Compensation for the appraiser cannot be related to a specific estimate of value ("I'll pay you $500 if you say the property is worth $150,000"), nor can the appraiser have an undisclosed interest in the property ("Come up with a good appraisal and you can act as a broker in the deal").

"AS IS" Agreement. A situation where property is sold without warranty and in whatever physical condition it may be in as of the time a contract is signed. Before entering such deals, both buyers and sellers should check state and local regulations and warranty rules to see if and how "AS IS" sales are affected by such laws.

Assumption. A situation where a buyer takes over loan payments and obligations from a seller. Both buyer and seller are responsible for repaying the entire debt if the purchaser defaults. Also see SUBJECT TO and FREELY ASSUMABLE.

Back Ratio. The proportion of purchaser income lenders will allow for principal, interest, taxes, insurance, and regular monthly debt when evaluating loan applications. See FRONT RATIO.

Balloon Notes. Real estate loans where some portion of the debt will remain unpaid at the end of the loan term. Second trusts, for example, are frequently short-term loans (say three to five years) where a single large payment is due when the loan ends. Often used with investment property in cases where buyers want low monthly payments.

Broker. A licensed real estate professional employed by a buyer or seller to assist in the purchase, sale, or management of real property. A broker's duties may include determining market values, advertising properties for sale, showing properties to prospective purchasers, assisting in the preparation of contracts, advising clients with regard to the acceptance or rejection of an offer or counter-offer, and dealing with a wide variety of related matters. While brokers have traditionally represented sellers, they can also be hired by purchasers, a concept known as "buyer brokerage." *For purposes of this guide, the term "broker" is often used in a general sense when either a broker or agent (or both) might be appropriate in certain situations.* For instance, a sentence saying that "Brokers frequently spend many weeks working with prospects" can just as easily apply to agents.

Buyer Broker. A real estate professional paid by, and representing, the purchaser alone.

Clear and Marketable Title. Property that can be sold immediately because all claims, such as existing mortgages, have been paid off, assumed, or otherwise cleared.

Closing. See SETTLEMENT.

Condominium.   When someone owns a "condo," they possess an individual property unit as well as a non-exclusive interest in the common areas controlled by the condominium organization.

Contingent Contract.   A contract with a qualification or condition which must be resolved before the contract is final.

Contingency.   A provision that makes a contract incomplete until a certain event occurs. For example, if investor Lanham offers to purchase the Hartford property "subject to a structural inspection satisfactory to Purchaser," there's no final contract unless Lanham says the structural inspection is satisfactory to him.

Contract.   In real estate, a binding, written agreement between two or more people to attain a common goal, typically the transfer of property ownership in exchange for money.

Cooperative.   When someone "owns" a co-op, they have stock in a corporation that owns real estate and the exclusive right to use a portion of the co-op's property.

Co-Owners.   Two or more people with an interest in a single parcel of property. An extremely important issue, since the form of co-ownership shown on a title may affect such matters as estates, inheritances, and personal liability in the event of a lawsuit.

Co-Signer.   A person who signs and assumes joint liability with another. For instance, Mr. Daly may co-sign a loan with his son. Note that a co-signer may share liability but that such an individual is not necessarily a co-owner.

Credit Report.   A report from an independent source which outlines a person's creditworthiness by listing debts, liabilities, assets, and related information. Used by lenders to assess the creditworthiness of potential borrowers. (*Note:* It's always a good idea to check your own credit report regularly to see that it's accurate. Contact local credit reporting agencies for more information.)

Curtailment.   A payment that shortens or ends a mortgage. For example, if an investor owes $25,000 on a mortgage and pays off the entire debt, the loan is said to be "curtailed."

Damages.   Compensation for loss or injury caused by another. Damages may be recovered by any person who has suffered loss, detriment, or injury through an unlawful act, omission, or negligent act of another.

Deed.   A document which transfers title to real estate from one party to another and is recorded among the governmental land records where the property is located.

Deferred Interest.   See NEGATIVE AMORTIZATION.

Deposit.   Usually money delivered by a buyer to a seller to assure that the buyer's contract obligations will be fulfilled.

Earnest Money.   See DEPOSIT.

Easement.   A right to use someone else's property. Beware, sometimes easements are created without an owner's permission or knowledge!

Encroachment.   An intrusion, obstruction, or invasion of someone else's property. For example, if a neighbor just built a fence and the fence is six inches over your property line, it's an encroachment.

Entitlement.   A right due to an individual. Used with VA mortgages. For instance, a $15,000 entitlement would mean that a vet could borrow that sum from a lender and the VA would guarantee its repayment. Since lenders usually want a 4:1 ratio between the value of an entitlement and the loan amount, having a $15,000 guarantee allows a borrower to receive a $60,000 loan.

Equity.   The cash value of property, less marketing expenses, after all liens have been paid off.

Escrow.   When money is held by one party for another it's usually placed in an "escrow" or trust account. For example, when an investor gives a broker a $10,000 deposit to purchase a house, that money is placed in an escrow account. The broker has no right to use the $10,000 for his own purposes.

Fair Market Value.   The price of a given property at a particular time as a result of negotiation between a knowledgeable buyer and seller.

Fixtures.   Items which usually convey to the buyer in a realty transaction unless specifically excluded from the sale. Fixtures are generally attached to the property and intended to be sold with it. Examples of common fixtures include built-in dishwashers, furnaces, chandeliers, and plumbing.

Freely Assumable Financing.   A loan which may be assumed by anyone without the lender's permission. With such financing, however, the original borrower normally remains liable if the loan is unpaid. This is not a problem in areas where home values are rising and a new purchaser has made a substantial down payment. In deals that involve little or no money down, and in areas where housing values are stable or falling, the risk to sellers may be substantial.

Front Ratio.   The proportion of purchaser income lenders will allow for principal, interest, taxes, and insurance when evaluating loan applications. See BACK RATIO.

Gift.   The voluntary transfer of money, property, or anything of value from one person to another without any duty or expectation of repayment. Since gifts in the context of a real estate transaction may be large, donors should check with a CPA or tax attorney before making a gift commitment to assure that all tax consequences are understood.

Income to Debt Ratio.   A measure used by lenders to determine if prospective borrowers are qualified for loans of a given size. For example, a lender might allow a borrower to use as much as

28 percent of his total monthly income to pay monthly costs for principal, interest, taxes, and insurance. The income-to-debt ratio is 28 to 100, or 28 percent.

Inspection.   An examination to determine condition or quality.

Installment Sale.   A transaction in which the buyer pays the seller in whole or in part after title has been transferred.

Junior Lien.   Much like shoppers in a supermarket line, lenders line up to be paid when a property is foreclosed. The order of repayment is established by the loan documents recorded in local governmental offices. The lender with the first claim has the first mortgage or first trust, the lender with the second claim holds the second mortgage or second trust, etc. If a loan is not a first trust or mortgage, it's a junior lien.

Language of Art (Legal Wording).   Standardized language with specific legal meanings. A trap for the unwary, legal language may contain definitions, meanings, shadings, and implications not found when the same words are used in everyday conversation.

Leverage.   A general investment concept meaning that you have been able to borrow and thereby use other people's money (OPM). If an investor buys property for $100,000, puts down $20,000 at settlement, and gets an $80,000 mortgage for the balance, his leverage is 1 to 4. If he only puts down $10,000 his leverage is 1 to 9, a better deal *if* the $10,000 he didn't put into the property can earn an equal or better return elsewhere *and* the property's value does not decline.

Liens.   A lien is a claim against property. Not only are mortgages and trusts liens, but overdue property taxes, unpaid repair bills, condo fees, and even water and sewage charges can all be liens. A major purpose of a title search is to be certain that all liens are known as of the day of settlement.

Loan Ap.   Industry jargon for "loan application."

Loan Origination Fee.   A fee charged by lenders to cover loan processing costs, often equal to 1 percent of the loan's value.

Loan-to-Value Ratio.   Used by virtually all lenders, the loan-to-value ratio, or LTV, compares the market value of a property with the amount of financing being sought. With conventional financing lenders seek an LTV of 80 percent—that is, property worth $10 for each $8 they lend.

Locking In.   Mortgage rates are widely advertised but the rate you see may not be your final rate at settlement, especially in a market where mortgage costs are rising. To assure a given rate at settlement, borrowers must often "lock in" rates by paying a fee when they apply for financing. Investors should be aware that lock-in arrangements may be subject to conditions that make them valueless; for example, a lock-in agreement that becomes invalid if market conditions change. Market conditions *always* change.

Merge.   To absorb or fuse one document or right into another. In real estate, this usually means the sales contract is merged into or becomes a part of the deed. Once this merger takes place, the real estate contract is no longer in effect. However, if a real estate contract says that a portion of the document—or the complete document—is to "survive," then that material will not be merged into the deed.

Multiple Listing System.   One: A marketing tool used within the real estate industry to disseminate information concerning a given property to a large number of agents and brokers. Two: A system of agency/sub-agency relationships. For example: if broker Dobbs lists a property for sale, Dobbs is the owner's agent. If broker Courtney sees the property in the multiple listing service and offers the property for sale, Courtney represents the owner as a sub-agent.

Negative Amortization.   A loan where monthly payments are too small to entirely pay for either principal or interest reductions, or both. For example, with a 30-year, $100,000 loan at 10 percent interest a self-amortizing loan will require monthly payments of $877.57. If the payments are only $800 the amortization statement will look like this:

Payment	Interest	Principal	Balance
#1	$800.00	−$33.33	$100,033.33
#2	$800.00	−$33.61	$100,066.94
#3	$800.00	−$33.89	$100,100.83
#4	$800.00	−$34.17	$100,135.00
Etc.			

Notice. A declaration or action that conspicuously identifies a condition, action, or non-action. For example, a statement that the basement leaks places a buyer "on notice" that a possibly harmful condition exists. Notice may also be unstated but presumed. For example, if a purchaser sees that the basement floor is wet, and if the seller has not attempted to hide the problem, then the buyer may be effectively on notice.

Offer. A proposal that, when accepted, will become a contract. In real estate the buyer commonly makes a written offer to purchase property which may then be accepted, rejected, or countered by the seller. Offers may be withdrawn without penalty at any time prior to acceptance, unless the offer provides otherwise. If a proposal is rejected it may not be resurrected without permission of the person who made the offer.

Option. A right to act under certain terms and conditions. For example, if Mr. Mullins can purchase the Butler property for $150,000 by June 1, he has an option. If he does not act by June 1, the option is dead. Note that Mullins need not wait for Butler to offer his property for sale or to accept an offer from another purchaser. See RIGHT OF FIRST REFUSAL.

Package Mortgage. A single mortgage used to acquire not only property but personal goods as well, such as a microwave oven.

Point (Loan Discount Fee).   An interest fee charged by lenders at settlement. One point is equal to 1 percent of a mortgage. The purpose of points is to raise the lender's yield above the apparent interest rate. May be paid by buyers, sellers, or both, though special rules may apply with some loans, such as FHA and VA mortgages.

Prime Rate.   Traditionally defined as the best rate available to a lender's best customers. More recently it is the subject of dispute because some borrowers have received rates below prime.

Principal, Interest, Taxes, and Insurance (PITI).   The four basic costs of homeownership that most concern lenders. For instance, a lender might say that a borrower could qualify for financing provided the PITI for a given mortgage does not exceed 28 percent of the individual's gross monthly income.

Quit-Claim Deed.   A deed which says, in effect, "Whatever title I have, if anything, I hereby give to you." Unfortunately, the seller who offers a quit-claim deed may have no rights or interests to sell. *Always consult an attorney before agreeing to any deal that involves a quit-claim deed.*

Refinance.   A situation where new financing is placed on a property. The addition of a second trust would be a *partial* refinancing. Replacing one loan with another would be a *total* refinancing.

Remedies.   Forms of compensation, such as money or actions, granted in response to a wrongful situation or condition.

Rent.   The economic cost to use someone else's property; or, seen from an owner's perspective, revenue derived from property ownership.

Right of First Refusal.   A priority right to purchase property under terms and conditions made by another purchaser and accepted by an owner. For example, if Hains offers $50,000 for the Wilshire property and Wilshire accepts the offer subject to Kean's right of first refusal, Kean has the right to buy the property for $50,000. Note that a right of first refusal may render a property less salable because marketability is clouded. Also see OPTION.

Satisfaction. Acceptance by one or both parties or the completion of an obligation. As an example, Mr. Brody offers to buy the Kent residence if he decides the roof inspection is satisfactory. If he accepts the inspection report the contract will be finalized.

Self-Amortization. When monthly payments for principal and interest allow a loan to be repaid over its term without any balloon payment, self-amortization has occurred.

Settlement (Closing). The act or process of adjusting and finalizing all dealings, money, and arrangements for real estate buyers and sellers. At settlement all debts are paid, all adjustments are made as of settlement, all money is properly disbursed, the deed is prepared with the new owner's name, and the property is conveyed in accordance with the contract and the intentions of the parties.

Subject To. An offer or contract which depends on a separate condition or action. In real estate, this phrase is usually found in a provision such as, "This property is sold subject to a right-of-way granted to the electric company allowing its electrical lines to cross the front yard."

Survey. An examination of property boundaries and related matters. A survey can reveal the quantity of land, boundary distances, where improvements are located, ground contours, and other vital information about the property.

Sweat Equity. Additional property value produced by an owner's time, labor, and intelligence. Unlike $1000 spent for a carpenter to add a deck, an owner's labor cannot be written off now or in the future when the property is sold.

Take Back. An expression that means a loan has been made directly to a purchaser by a seller, as in, "Seller Griffin will take back a $50,000 second trust from Buyer Landow."

Tenancies.   Interests in real estate defined in the deed. A vitally important matter which shows how title to the property is held.

Tenant.   An individual or entity, such as a business, that occupies someone else's property. Note that while *tenancies* usually describe forms of property ownership, a *tenant* does not own property.

Termites.   Wood-boring insects that can infest and damage homes. Most realty sales require a termite inspection showing the property is free and clear of termites and other wood-boring insects. Such inspections should also list insect damage, if any.

Timesharing.   A form of activity where a single property is used by multiple owners. Note that timesharing does not necessarily refer to real estate ownership; some timeshare units are vacation leases or merely a right to use certain facilities. Note also that since timeshare financing is often in the form of a personal loan rather than debt secured by real property, timeshare interest may be regarded as consumer debt rather than tax-deductible real estate interest.

Title.   The right of property ownership. Such ownership can be held solely, jointly, in common, or in corporate or partnership form. A person who holds a vested interest in real estate is said to hold title whether he holds it for himself or for others.

Title Insurance.   Policies purchased at settlement which insure that one's ownership or interest in the property is protected against loss if a title defect is found or if title claims are made after ownership is transferred. Policies differ and may contain exclusions and exceptions. Also, policy coverage may be expanded to include additional protection. Speak to the person conducting settlement for complete information.

Warranties.   Guarantees, promises, and protections provided by one party to another. In real estate contracts there are usually warranties regarding the condition of appliances and certain fixtures. New homes often have extensive warranties covering not only fixtures and appliances but the overall structure as well. There can be *express* (written) warranties and *implied* warranties, guarantees that the parties intended even though they may not have stated them specifically in the contract.

Zoning.   Rules for land use established by local governments.

Appendix B

Amortization Statement

One of the most important documents in every real estate transaction is the amortization statement, a schedule that shows how monthly mortgage payments are divided between principal and interest, and also how much debt remains outstanding at the end of each month.

The following amortization statement describes how a $90,000 loan with a 10 percent interest rate will be paid out over 30 years. The figures are approximate, but they demonstrate that relatively little principal is repaid during the loan's first years. In fact, after ten years—a full one-third of the loan term—the mortgage balance has only been reduced by $8,155.

The amortization statement presented here shows what happens with a fixed-rate loan over 30 years. ARM borrowers cannot predict future costs with such certainty, because ARM payments and rates can fluctuate. With ARMs, worst-case scenarios can be used to show how the loans will behave in extreme conditions, conditions that may not be realistic or reasonable.

For information concerning individual loans, be certain to consult with specific lenders for complete details.

Amortization Statement

Loan Amount	$90,000
Interest	10 percent
Number of Years	30
Monthly Payment	$789.81
Total Interest Cost	$194,331.60

Payment	Interest Payment	Principal Payment	Balance Due
1	750.00	39.81	89,960.19
2	749.67	40.14	89,920.05
3	749.33	40.48	89,879.57
4	749.00	40.81	89,838.76
5	748.66	41.15	89,797.60
6	748.31	41.50	89,756.11
7	747.97	41.84	89,714.27
8	747.62	42.19	89,672.07
9	747.27	42.54	89,629.53
10	746.91	42.90	89,586.63
11	746.56	43.25	89,543.38
12	746.19	43.62	89,499.76
Year 1	8,977.48	500.24	89,499.76
13	745.83	43.98	89,455.79
14	745.46	44.35	89,411.44
15	745.10	44.71	89,366.73
16	744.72	45.09	89,321.64
17	744.35	45.46	89,276.18
18	743.97	45.84	89,230.33
19	743.59	46.22	89,184.11
20	743.20	46.61	89,137.50
21	742.81	47.00	89,090.50
22	742.42	47.39	89,043.11
23	742.03	47.78	88,995.33
24	741.63	48.18	88,947.15
Year 2	8,925.10	552.62	88,947.15
25	741.23	48.58	88,898.56
26	740.82	48.99	88,849.58
27	740.41	49.40	88,800.18

Payment	Interest Payment	Principal Payment	Balance Due
28	740.00	49.81	88,750.37
29	739.59	50.22	88,700.15
30	739.17	50.64	88,649.50
31	738.75	51.06	88,598.44
32	738.32	51.49	88,546.95
33	737.89	51.92	88,495.03
34	737.46	52.35	88,442.68
35	737.02	52.79	88,389.89
36	736.58	53.23	88,336.67
Year 3	8,867.24	610.48	88,336.67
37	736.14	53.67	88,282.99
38	735.69	54.12	88,228.88
39	735.24	54.57	88,174.31
40	734.79	55.02	88,119.28
41	734.33	55.48	88,063.80
42	733.87	55.94	88,007.86
43	733.40	56.41	87,951.44
44	732.93	56.88	87,894.56
45	732.45	57.36	87,837.21
46	731.98	57.83	87,779.37
47	731.49	58.32	87,721.06
48	731.01	58.80	87,662.26
Year 4	8,803.31	674.41	87,662.26
49	730.52	59.29	87,602.97
50	730.02	59.79	87,543.18
51	729.53	60.28	87,482.90
52	729.02	60.79	87,422.11
53	728.52	61.29	87,360.82
54	728.01	61.80	87,299.02
55	727.49	62.32	87,236.70
56	726.97	62.84	87,173.86
57	726.45	63.36	87,110.50
58	725.92	63.89	87,046.61

Amortization Statement

Payment	Interest Payment	Principal Payment	Balance Due
59	725.39	64.42	86,982.19
60	724.85	64.96	86,917.23
Year 5	8,732.69	745.03	86,917.23
61	724.31	65.50	86,851.73
62	723.76	66.05	86,785.68
63	723.21	66.60	86,719.09
64	722.66	67.15	86,651.94
65	722.10	67.71	86,584.23
66	721.54	68.27	86,515.95
67	720.97	68.84	86,447.11
68	720.39	69.42	86,377.69
69	719.81	70.00	86,307.70
70	719.23	70.58	86,237.12
71	718.64	71.17	86,165.95
72	718.05	71.76	86,094.19
Year 6	8,654.68	823.04	86,094.19
73	717.45	72.36	86,021.83
74	716.85	72.96	85,948.87
75	716.24	73.57	85,875.30
76	715.63	74.18	85,801.12
77	715.01	74.80	85,726.32
78	714.39	75.42	85,650.89
79	713.76	76.05	85,574.84
80	713.12	76.69	85,498.15
81	712.48	77.33	85,420.83
82	711.84	77.97	85,342.86
83	711.19	78.62	85,264.24
84	710.54	79.27	85,184.96
Year 7	8,568.50	909.22	85,184.96
85	709.87	79.94	85,105.03
86	709.21	80.60	85,024.43
87	708.54	81.27	84,943.15

Payment	Interest Payment	Principal Payment	Balance Due
88	707.86	81.95	84,861.20
89	707.18	82.63	84,778.57
90	706.49	83.32	84,695.25
91	705.79	84.02	84,611.23
92	705.09	84.72	84,526.52
93	704.39	85.42	84,441.09
94	703.68	86.13	84,354.96
95	702.96	86.85	84,268.11
96	702.23	87.58	84,180.53
Year 8	8,473.29	1,004.43	84,180.53
97	701.50	88.31	84,092.23
98	700.77	89.04	84,003.18
99	700.03	89.78	83,913.40
100	699.28	90.53	83,822.87
101	698.52	91.29	83,731.58
102	697.76	92.05	83,639.54
103	697.00	92.81	83,546.72
104	696.22	93.59	83,453.14
105	695.44	94.37	83,358.77
106	694.66	95.15	83,263.61
107	693.86	95.95	83,167.67
108	693.06	96.75	83,070.92
Year 9	8,368.11	1,109.61	83,070.92
109	692.26	97.55	82,973.37
110	691.44	98.37	82,875.00
111	690.63	99.18	82,775.82
112	689.80	100.01	82,675.81
113	688.97	100.84	82,574.96
114	688.12	101.69	82,473.28
115	687.28	102.53	82,370.74
116	686.42	103.39	82,267.36
117	685.56	104.25	82,163.11
118	684.69	105.12	82,057.99

Payment	Interest Payment	Principal Payment	Balance Due
119	683.82	105.99	81,952.00
120	682.93	106.88	81,845.12
Year 10	8,251.92	1,225.80	81,845.12
121	682.04	107.77	81,737.35
122	681.14	108.67	81,628.69
123	680.24	109.57	81,519.12
124	679.33	110.48	81,408.63
125	678.41	111.40	81,297.23
126	677.48	112.33	81,184.90
127	676.54	113.27	81,071.63
128	675.60	114.21	80,957.41
129	674.65	115.16	80,842.25
130	673.69	116.12	80,726.12
131	672.72	117.09	80,609.03
132	671.74	118.07	80,490.96
Year 11	8,123.56	1,354.16	80,490.96
133	670.76	119.05	80,371.91
134	669.77	120.04	80,251.87
135	668.77	121.04	80,130.82
136	667.76	122.05	80,008.77
137	666.74	123.07	79,885.70
138	665.71	124.10	79,761.60
139	664.68	125.13	79,636.47
140	663.64	126.17	79,510.30
141	662.59	127.22	79,383.08
142	661.53	128.28	79,254.79
143	660.46	129.35	79,125.44
144	659.38	130.43	78,995.01
Year 12	7,981.76	1,495.96	78,995.01
145	658.29	131.52	78,863.49
146	657.20	132.61	78,730.88
147	656.09	133.72	78,597.16

Payment	Interest Payment	Principal Payment	Balance Due
148	654.98	134.83	78,462.32
149	653.85	135.96	78,326.37
150	652.72	137.09	78,189.27
151	651.58	138.23	78,051.04
152	650.43	139.38	77,911.66
153	649.26	140.55	77,771.11
154	648.09	141.72	77,629.39
155	646.91	142.90	77,486.50
156	645.72	144.09	77,342.41
Year 13	7,825.12	1,652.60	77,342.41
157	644.52	145.29	77,197.12
158	643.31	146.50	77,050.62
159	642.09	147.72	76,902.89
160	640.86	148.95	76,753.94
161	639.62	150.19	76,603.75
162	638.36	151.45	76,452.30
163	637.10	152.71	76,299.59
164	635.83	153.98	76,145.61
165	634.55	155.26	75,990.35
166	633.25	156.56	75,833.79
167	631.95	157.86	75,675.93
168	630.63	159.18	75,516.76
Year 14	7,652.07	1,825.65	75,516.76
169	629.31	160.50	75,356.25
170	627.97	161.84	75,194.41
171	626.62	163.19	75,031.22
172	625.26	164.55	74,866.67
173	623.89	165.92	74,700.75
174	622.51	167.30	74,533.45
175	621.11	168.70	74,364.75
176	619.71	170.10	74,194.64
177	618.29	171.52	74,023.12
178	616.86	172.95	73,850.17

Payment	Interest Payment	Principal Payment	Balance Due
179	615.42	174.39	73,675.78
180	613.96	175.85	73,499.94
Year 15	7,460.90	2,016.82	73,499.94
181	612.50	177.31	73,322.63
182	611.02	178.79	73,143.84
183	609.53	180.28	72,963.56
184	608.03	181.78	72,781.78
185	606.51	183.30	72,598.49
186	604.99	184.82	72,413.67
187	603.45	186.36	72,227.30
188	601.89	187.92	72,039.39
189	600.33	189.48	71,849.91
190	598.75	191.06	71,658.84
191	597.16	192.65	71,466.19
192	595.55	194.26	71,271.93
Year 16	7,249.71	2,228.01	71,271.93
193	593.93	195.88	71,076.06
194	592.30	197.51	70,878.55
195	590.65	199.16	70,679.39
196	588.99	200.82	70,478.58
197	587.32	202.49	70,276.09
198	585.63	204.18	70,071.91
199	583.93	205.88	69,866.03
200	582.22	207.59	69,658.44
201	580.49	209.32	69,449.12
202	578.74	211.07	69,238.05
203	576.98	212.83	69,025.22
204	575.21	214.60	68,810.62
Year 17	7,016.41	2,461.31	68,810.62
205	573.42	216.39	68,594.24
206	571.62	218.19	68,376.04
207	569.80	220.01	68,156.04

Payment	Interest Payment	Principal Payment	Balance Due
208	567.97	221.84	67,934.19
209	566.12	223.69	67,710.50
210	564.25	225.56	67,484.94
211	562.37	227.44	67,257.51
212	560.48	229.33	67,028.18
213	558.57	231.24	66,796.94
214	556.64	233.17	66,563.77
215	554.70	235.11	66,328.66
216	552.74	237.07	66,091.58
Year 18	6,758.68	2,719.04	66,091.58
217	550.76	239.05	65,852.54
218	548.77	241.04	65,611.50
219	546.76	243.05	65,368.45
220	544.74	245.07	65,123.38
221	542.69	247.12	64,876.26
222	540.64	249.17	64,627.09
223	538.56	251.25	64,375.84
224	536.47	253.34	64,122.49
225	534.35	255.46	63,867.04
226	532.23	257.58	63,609.45
227	530.08	259.73	63,349.72
228	527.91	261.90	63,087.83
Year 19	6,473.96	3,003.76	63,087.83
229	525.73	264.08	62,823.75
230	523.53	266.28	62,557.47
231	521.31	268.50	62,288.97
232	519.07	270.74	62,018.24
233	516.82	272.99	61,745.24
234	514.54	275.27	61,469.98
235	512.25	277.56	61,192.42
236	509.94	279.87	60,912.54
237	507.60	282.21	60,630.34
238	505.25	284.56	60,345.78

Payment	Interest Payment	Principal Payment	Balance Due
239	502.88	286.93	60,058.85
240	500.49	289.32	59,769.53
Year 20	6,159.43	3,318.29	59,769.53
241	498.08	291.73	59,477.80
242	495.65	294.16	59,183.64
243	493.20	296.61	58,887.03
244	490.73	299.08	58,587.94
245	488.23	301.58	58,286.37
246	485.72	304.09	57,982.28
247	483.19	306.62	57,675.65
248	480.63	309.18	57,366.47
249	478.05	311.76	57,054.72
250	475.46	314.35	56,740.36
251	472.84	316.97	56,423.39
252	470.19	319.62	56,103.77
Year 21	5,811.96	3,665.76	56,103.77
253	467.53	322.28	55,781.50
254	464.85	324.96	55,456.53
255	462.14	327.67	55,128.86
256	459.41	330.40	54,798.46
257	456.65	333.16	54,465.30
258	453.88	335.93	54,129.37
259	451.08	338.73	53,790.64
260	448.26	341.55	53,449.08
261	445.41	344.40	53,104.68
262	442.54	347.27	52,757.41
263	439.65	350.16	52,407.24
264	436.73	353.08	52,054.16
Year 22	5,428.11	4,049.61	52,054.16
265	433.78	356.03	51,698.14
266	430.82	358.99	51,339.14
267	427.83	361.98	50,977.16

Payment	Interest Payment	Principal Payment	Balance Due
268	424.81	365.00	50,612.16
269	421.77	368.04	50,244.12
270	418.70	371.11	49,873.01
271	415.61	374.20	49,498.81
272	412.49	377.32	49,121.49
273	409.35	380.46	48,741.02
274	406.18	383.63	48,357.39
275	402.98	386.83	47,970.56
276	399.75	390.06	47,580.50
Year 23	5,004.06	4,473.66	47,580.50
277	396.50	393.31	47,187.19
278	393.23	396.58	46,790.61
279	389.92	399.89	46,390.72
280	386.59	403.22	45,987.50
281	383.23	406.58	45,580.92
282	379.84	409.97	45,170.95
283	376.42	413.39	44,757.57
284	372.98	416.83	44,340.74
285	369.51	420.30	43,920.43
286	366.00	423.81	43,496.63
287	362.47	427.34	43,069.29
288	358.91	430.90	42,638.39
Year 24	4,535.61	4,942.11	42,638.39
289	355.32	434.49	42,203.90
290	351.70	438.11	41,765.79
291	348.05	441.76	41,324.03
292	344.37	445.44	40,878.58
293	340.65	449.16	40,429.43
294	336.91	452.90	39,976.53
295	333.14	456.67	39,519.86
296	329.33	460.48	39,059.38
297	325.49	464.32	38,595.06
298	321.63	468.18	38,126.88

Payment	Interest Payment	Principal Payment	Balance Due
299	317.72	472.09	37,654.79
300	313.79	476.02	37,178.77
Year 25	4,018.11	5,459.61	37,178.77
301	309.82	479.99	36,698.79
302	305.82	483.99	36,214.80
303	301.79	488.02	35,726.78
304	297.72	492.09	35,234.69
305	293.62	496.19	34,738.51
306	289.49	500.32	34,238.18
307	285.32	504.49	33,733.69
308	281.11	508.70	33,225.00
309	276.87	512.94	32,712.06
310	272.60	517.21	32,194.85
311	268.29	521.52	31,673.33
312	263.94	525.87	31,147.47
Year 26	3,446.41	6,031.31	31,147.47
313	259.56	530.25	30,617.22
314	255.14	534.67	30,082.55
315	250.69	539.12	29,543.43
316	246.20	543.61	28,999.82
317	241.67	548.14	28,451.67
318	237.10	552.71	27,898.96
319	232.49	557.32	27,341.64
320	227.85	561.96	26,779.68
321	223.16	566.65	26,213.03
322	218.44	571.37	25,641.66
323	213.68	576.13	25,065.53
324	208.88	580.93	24,484.60
Year 27	2,814.86	6,662.86	24,484.60
325	204.04	585.77	23,898.83
326	199.16	590.65	23,308.18
327	194.23	595.58	22,712.60

Payment	Interest Payment	Principal Payment	Balance Due
328	189.27	600.54	22,112.06
329	184.27	605.54	21,506.52
330	179.22	610.59	20,895.93
331	174.13	615.68	20,280.25
332	169.00	620.81	19,659.45
333	163.83	625.98	19,033.47
334	158.61	631.20	18,402.27
335	153.35	636.46	17,765.81
336	148.05	641.76	17,124.05
Year 28	2,117.17	7,360.55	17,124.05
337	142.70	647.11	16,476.94
338	137.31	652.50	15,824.44
339	131.87	657.94	15,166.50
340	126.39	663.42	14,503.07
341	120.86	668.95	13,834.12
342	115.28	674.53	13,159.60
343	109.66	680.15	12,479.45
344	104.00	685.81	11,793.64
345	98.28	691.53	11,102.11
346	92.52	697.29	10,404.81
347	86.71	703.10	9,701.71
348	80.85	708.96	8,992.75
Year 29	1,346.42	8,131.30	8,992.75
349	74.94	714.87	8,277.88
350	68.98	720.83	7,557.05
351	62.98	726.83	6,830.22
352	56.92	732.89	6,097.32
353	50.81	739.00	5,358.33
354	44.65	745.16	4,613.17
355	38.44	751.37	3,861.80
356	32.18	757.63	3,104.17
357	25.87	763.94	2,340.23
358	19.50	770.31	1,569.92

Payment	Interest Payment	Principal Payment	Balance Due
359	13.08	776.73	793.20
360	6.61	783.20	10.00
Year 30	494.97	8,982.75	10.00

Index

213